'... musical stories to guide us through our emotional lives.'
Baz Luhrmann

'I would like to issue a caution: Mr Lawrence is peddling a dangerous substance here. If you take too much of this Swoon you could become a swoon loon – staggering down the street, a head full of swoon tunes.'
Richard Tognetti

'"I am afraid there are moments in life when even Schubert has nothing to say to us. We must admit, however, that they are our worst." So says Madame Merle from Henry James' Portrait of a Lady. Christopher Lawrence gives readers and listeners more chance to respond to the intrigue – this perfection of harmony of voice and instrument which is at the centre of the deeply felt human need for music. This book, which can be carried and read, opened and closed and reopened at the will of fortunate owners is the gift of a lifetime.'
Elizabeth Jolley

SWOONING

SWOONING

**A CLASSICAL MUSIC GUIDE TO
LIFE, LOVE, LUST AND OTHER FOLLIES**

CHRISTOPHER LAWRENCE

Published by Nero,
an imprint of Schwartz Publishing Pty Ltd
37–39 Langridge Street
Collingwood VIC 3066, Australia
enquiries@blackincbooks.com
www.nerobooks.com

Copyright © Christopher Lawrence 2001
This revised edition published 2015
Christopher Lawrence asserts his right to be known as the author of this work.

ALL RIGHTS RESERVED.
No part of this publication may be reproduced, stored in a retrieval system, or transmitted in any form by any means electronic, mechanical, photocopying, recording or otherwise without the prior consent of the publishers.

National Library of Australia Cataloguing-in-Publication entry:
Lawrence, Christopher, author.
Swooning : a classical music guide to life, love, lust, and other follies
Second edition.
9781863957502 (paperback)
9781925203677 (ebook)
Music–Anecdotes. Composers–Anecdotes.
Musicians–Anecdotes. Music–Psychological aspects.
781.68

Cover design by Peter Long
Text design by Tristan Main

swoon (*swun*)

verb
    1. a literary word meaning to faint/lose consciousness
    2. to enter a state of ecstasy

noun
    3. a fainting fit
    4. a piece of classical music that induces profound emotional reaction
    (origin: Australian radio segment, c1994)

Preparatory Upbeat

You've heard of the film based on the book, or the musical based on the play. What you have here is a little different: the book about classical music based on the feeling it inspires. It is also a book about a subject most agree words cannot describe, and whose continuing pleasures would be unknown to the person who literally followed the title's command. You don't hear very much if you have passed out.

Therein lies all the illogicality of a brand, as a little radio segment that I started back in the last century has become. But what a product! Many of the most beautiful ideas people have ever had and – at a time when our means to express or even contemplate a personal narrative have been condensed down to quotidian banalities on a social media page – a ticket to ride a sound or voice or melody all the way to the farthest corner of ourselves. It is a marvellous thing to do, perhaps the most purely creative thing you will do all day. People have asked me for years why this casual little moniker, applied to a piece of music, struck such a chord (sorry), and the best I can come up with by way of reply is that deep down, we are all poets. Yes, that's *you*.

The reappearance of *Swooning* in paperback is flattering, if surprising. Surely if books with even the faintest whiff of 'self-help' were truly successful, they would never be seen again: mission accomplished. On the other hand, the music that silently swirls through these pages has enjoyed a fabulous shelf life by modern retail standards, and no obsolescence is planned. Mozart doesn't expire at the end of the month. Tchaikovsky 1.0 hardly requires an upgrade. The thing about the classics is that *we* are the passing parade, and in the years since this book's first release many more people, having stumbled upon a bit of classical music they quite like, wouldn't mind getting more advice on how to make some other proverbial pennies drop.

As I explain herein, this little book doesn't aspire to teach you the 'how'. That sort of explanation is for more technical tomes. Even then there are no guarantees. Igor Stravinsky, whose ballet *The Rite of Spring* sparked a chair-brandishing riot in 1913, famously said 'I haven't understood a bar of music in my life, but I have felt it'. Thanks a lot, Igor. If the subject stumps one of the brainiest composers of all time, what hope is there for the rest of us? For him, too, it came down to feelings, and that is where *Swooning* will take you. A menu of such intangible matters hardly merits a 'contents' page, but since you are invited to the Concert of Life over the next few hours, we can at least offer you a programme.

YOUR PROGRAMME

MAKING OVERTURES 1

LOVE 9
Hector Berlioz and the two wings of the soul

LUST 33
Tutti, meaning something for everybody

EXCESS & OBSESSION 55
Percy Grainger and his single interest

TRIUMPH 85
Richard Wagner and why the world
owed him a living

JOY 105
Emmanuel Chabrier and the profundity of frivolity

INTERVAL
During which you will be offered
a fine selection of

SOME MUSICAL LIFE TIPS 119

ANGER 143
Ludwig van Beethoven and the incident of the plate

SADNESS 165
Peter Tchaikovsky and the beauty of tears

FREEDOM & RELEASE 181
Wolfgang Amadeus Mozart and the kick up the arse

HOPE 199
Ross Edwards and the courage in change

PEACE 219
Hildegard of Bingen and the flying feather

CODA 231

~

THIS BOOK WILL CONCLUDE WITH
ACKNOWLEDGEMENTS AT 10.30.

IT IS REQUESTED THAT THE READER REFRAIN
FROM SWOONING IN THE AISLES AS THIS MAY
DISTRESS THE PERFORMERS.

MAKING OVERTURES

'Music was invented to deceive and delude mankind.'
Ephorus (4th century BC)

There's no denying it: music has this way of getting under the cranium and really stirring things around. Over the course of thousands of years many have marvelled at, or deplored, its seductive power. Ever since rocks were banged in rhythm, lips pursed to bamboo, or strands of sheep gut strung within a wooden frame and plucked, listening to music has delivered more than the occasional challenge to reason.

Conversely, its power as a harnesser of mass feeling is beyond question – ask any football crowd. If religion is truly the opiate of the masses, then music is the cigarette holder. Even on an individual basis the hypnotism works. At vulnerable moments of solitude, people can burst into spontaneous tears at the cue of a haunting refrain. Distant memories resurface; long-forgotten chapters in our lives are replayed. We become who we were. Other feelings that seem to have no connection to our direct experience well up and threaten to overwhelm us: pure wonder, all-encompassing joy, or an existential melancholy ripe for wallowing.

At other times we may be persuaded by a serene piece of music to cast emotion aside in favour of the contemplation of less corporeal concerns; at the very least, to stop whatever we are doing for a few minutes. I can testify to this having happened on a daily basis when I presented the breakfast shift for a national classical music radio program in Australia. Listeners were invited to 'swoon', and the invitation soon became the segment's title.

The early morning pause for a *Swoon* became a ritual for many thousands of people. Toast would be served in time for listening to something mellow, the scraping of the Vegemite following the slow rhythm of an ancient Armenian chant. Train passengers would bring peace and compassion to the rest of the carriage, courtesy of a soulful soprano aria leaking through headphones. Drivers looked dreamily at the vehicle alongside in commuter gridlock and lingered in the car park at the end of the journey, windows wound up to seal in the ripple of Venetian

Baroque. We were told that some people died calmly and more than a few were conceived during those highly anticipated minutes.

We had joked about serving a regular 'parcel of rapture', but the joke was on us. It seemed that we were performing a true public service, or at least fulfilling some deep need in many people; so deep, in fact, that they soon wanted more than a tiny weekday dosage. It was time for *Swoon* on tap, and the first of the CD compilations of 'greatest hits' from the segment was issued.

We were rashly optimistic about the first of the *Swoon* collections and manufactured 5,000 copies for sale around Australia. Even today, more so than in 1995, classical releases sell a fraction of that figure, yet we hoped that regular radio exposure would give the CDs an extra kick along. It obviously helped: over four years, the initial release was followed by two more and sales of the series soared to over half a million units, bringing each one both Gold and Platinum award status and making them the highest-selling classical compilations ever released Down Under. Radio exposure aside, this *Swoon* phenomenon had to have another explanation.

One reason for this success was undoubtedly the title, signalling an appropriate mode of response. In showbiz parlance, it was the 'hook'. But that's not all. Most of us have some untouched emotional buttons hidden away. It should therefore come as no surprise that classical music can (*ahem*) play us like a violin. How does this happen?

I believe that great music presents us with a sense of the universality of human experience, a reminder that when the composers were in full communicative flight they were, after all, talking about *us*: our longings, our desire for romance, our capacity for excess, and our wish for the eternal. Why, then, do many find this music – the masterpieces of Beethoven, Bach, Mozart and the rest of the periwigged gang – so inscrutable, when the conduct of the composers' own lives is so resoundingly familiar? Granted, the craft of writing music requires great discipline. But take the composers away from their ink-splattered pages and the same old patterns of behavioural ineptitude begin to take shape. The capacity to write great music seems not to be a talent for living. Classical music – *nice*? Not often: it is the most immediate expression of mental and emotional extremes, part deception (as Ephorus would have it), sometimes dangerous, and frequently a discomforting revelation.

Just as the unsuspecting listener makes the connections between classical music and certain states of mind, so this book clusters fact, rumination and trivia into sections corresponding roughly with the sequence of emotions experienced in a love affair. We're familiar with each of these stages – they bring out the best and worst of us – and classical music derives much of its inspiration from them too, leading us back through their tortuous terrain.

Just as in a nature walk the flowers remarked upon today are not the ones chosen tomorrow, *Swooning* pleads a case for arbitrariness. Inevitably, I have charted my own idiosyncratic path through the mountains of data that populate this vast musical-historical landscape (really, life is too short for some biographies) and there is the unmistakable feel of the scrapbook in the arrangement of material under these headings. Each section will also include a close-up of a composer whose life exemplifies the emotional 'subject' in question. Like everything else in the book, these life stories are not remotely authoritative, being at best an anecdotal recounting of fact; neither is there the intention to list the ten 'best' composers. Their presence here is the author's indulgence; they are composers who have meant a great deal to me and to whose music I have been irresistibly drawn. In explaining the nature of that attraction I hope to promote an interest through example that might inspire you to chase up the music and lives of other great composers, or to listen again to works that slipped by without notice. Another time, there will be so many more people to meet and stories to tell. Consider this Volume One.

Our cast of fellow sufferers in this book is drawn mainly from the 'Romantic' period in nineteenth-century Europe. They wanted emotion in music to be an art form, after all.

Just one living composer is included, and it is only because I know him well that I feel I can speak about him with such arrant presumption.

'There is nothing more difficult than talking about music.'
                                    Camille Saint-Saens (1835–1921)

And that's putting it mildly. Others have considered it an exercise in futility, culminating in the famous saying attributed to everyone from Thelonius Monk to Elvis Costello along the lines of writing about music being like 'dancing about architecture'. Since this book in no way constitutes a serious attempt to resolve the problem, I freely admit there *is* an irrelevance about trying to 'explain' music when music is 'about' something that words aren't. The world is full of maxims that concern music starting where the word leaves off. Many (our new friend Igor Stravinsky among them) maintain that music doesn't express anything at all. Perhaps not in any objective sense, but I've been serving music up to people for a long time, and the experience has taught me that music is about what it means to us, what it stirs in *you*. At first hearing we intuitively relate it to our emotional selves. If we find that we can't do this for whatever reason – the language is unintelligible, the person next to us is snoring, the iTunes replay keeps putting in gaps at track cue points – we lose patience with it and move on. The actual responses can't be moulded, but the patience and application can. This is where a word or two might be handy.

Words about music for the novice can be had in what is called a 'music appreciation' course. This is such an awful term. Learning to 'appreciate' good music is a bit like learning to sift patiently through your spouse's personality in search of the odd redeeming feature in an arranged marriage. Of course many arranged marriages do work out, but only after the partners reach an accommodation with each other. These days we don't want to spend twenty years learning to accommodate a Beethoven symphony.

What we're really after is fulfilment with a bit of romance and excitement along the way. This is as true of people as it is of symphonies, sonatas and operas. We're not just encountering Beethoven, we're meeting him on a speed date, so first impressions mean a lot. Eventually one learns to look or listen beneath the surface to the goodness within. It does help, however, to have been just a little captivated over the first dinner.

My self-declared task, therefore, is to introduce you to a few friends like, say, Tchaikovsky, and point out a few things he and you might have in common before leaving you both to talk. What I *won't* do is to tell you how you should listen to Tchaikovsky's Fifth Symphony; just as I won't try to tell you what (if anything) the Symphony is about, or indeed how Tchaikovsky went about writing it. That would be an attempt to write seriously about music, and in a funny way this isn't really a book about music at all. There will be plenty of advice, none of it couched in philosophical terms. Philosophy tries to come up with solutions, whereas we'll just be looking at problems.

No, this is a book about life, or to be more specific, the feelings, tastes, aversions and cravings of an inner life. When we listen to great music, we juxtapose our life experience with that of the composer. The junction points that are created can bring us miraculously face-to-face with the people who've been good enough to send out these musical messages.

Welcome to the wide, wild and wise world of classical music from the point of view of only one serious and lifelong music lover. The orchestra has tuned, the lights in the hall have dimmed, and the conductor's baton signals the downbeat for the beginning of the romance. Settle back – it's telling you something.

LOVE

'Love cannot give an idea of music, but music can give an idea of love.'

Hector Berlioz, 1865

That quote by Berlioz is the inspiration for this book, so let us begin our *Swoon* with that magic moment, when your eyes meet across a crowded room and you hear a thousand violins. How Romantic – and in the case of the French composer Hector Berlioz (1803–1869), a maxim shaped by a lifetime's experience.

    I first heard the music of Berlioz when I was twelve, after an exploration of the family collection of Broadway musical soundtracks, Judy Garland concerts, Herb Alpert and Sergio Mendes, and early Beatles. My tinkering at the piano had included some of J.S. Bach's two-part inventions and the odd simplified minuet. From there I began delving into classical music by scrounging money from my musician father to buy a cheap series of ten-inch vinyl LPs that came out each week under the title *The Great Composers,* which included an accompanying booklet detailing the composer's life, sometimes with a portrait on the cover.

It was his face that grabbed me. Most of the composers had been portrayed with expressions ranging from complacent satisfaction to inner glow. These guys knew they were good and so, too, did the world. From this I concluded that talent inevitably earned universal approbation. (Maturity proved me wrong). Sure, Beethoven looked a little wild-eyed towards the end, but I figured that was the drink.

Then came the Berlioz instalment. Wow, I thought, this guy's a little left-of-field: his name ends with a 'z'. Underneath this headline I saw the Gustave Courbet portrait from 1850 that somehow has more immediacy than a mere photographic image from life, showing a tense face against a dark background. Deep-set eyes gaze warily, almost suspiciously, at the viewer. My physiognomical instincts told me this was not a happy man.

Hang on: this guy was probably a genius, I reasoned. With a brain like that, Berlioz should have been ecstatic. Being a kid in the euphoric sixties, it never occurred to me that people had to suffer for their Art. From what I'd seen, being talented in music or art meant that you could dress and behave strangely and be rewarded with money and fame. What was this Frenchman's problem?

The answer was on the disc. It was a symphony, but not a numbered piece like Beethoven's ninth, Mozart's forty-first or Haydn's hundred-and-fourth. Instead, it had a name: the *Symphonie fantastique* (or *Fantastic Symphony*), with each of its five movements also bearing a title, beginning with the state of mind of *Rêveries – Passions*. This was of obvious appeal to someone on the hormonal cusp and I was keen to hear what Berlioz had to say about it.

The gramophone needle slid into the groove and the music began, and I hope that everyone has the chance just once in their lives to feel a connection with a creative artist that goes beyond mere aesthetic understanding or intellectual accord and arrives at something deeper: a real intuitive link, the sense that this person is singing your song as well as their own. The opening tune of the symphony is so suffused with longing, so *lonely*, that it shrugs off the comfort of any supporting rhythm. Even the accompaniment is cautious.

Berlioz stated that this opening was 'the expression of that overpowering sadness felt by a young heart first tortured by hopeless love'. I hadn't yet experienced such torture, but if it felt this beautiful, bring it on. The symphony was the soundtrack to a romantic drama for which

Berlioz supplied a lurid story, or 'programme'. In today's language of the tabloids it might read

> # HEADLESS MUSICIAN CONFRONTS WITCH GIRLFRIEND AT DIABOLICAL ORGY AFTER DRUG OVERDOSE!

And that's just the last two movements. No wonder they loved it in Paris in 1830. This was the 'Fantastic' of the title, a conflation of fantastical settings with a story of love gone wrong. This is precisely what a new generation of composers, artists and writers were after in the early nineteenth century. For them, 'Romantic' connoted something wild, fanciful and strange. Long before teenagers screamed and fainted at Elvis, Berlioz and sundry other Paris-based passion heads like Victor Hugo and Alexandre Dumas wept and vomited over Shakespeare. The Bard's poetry gushed with the lava of real life, even for those with little or no English.

The conduct of one's life could echo this new perception of Art, and the history of Berlioz's love life, like the story of his first symphony, proves that being a Romantic is not a guarantee of happiness. In his case, five overlapping love stories played through to unhappy ends over a span of fifty years:

BERLIOZ – HONEY, I GOT IT WRONG AGAIN

1816 Berlioz falls in love with Estelle (1), his eighteen-year-old neighbour and family friend. There's nothing transient about this adolescent passion; she becomes one of the themes of his life. For the time being there is no real future in this one. She thinks him merely cute. He's only twelve.

1827 Now an impoverished music student, Berlioz attends performances of Shakespeare's *Hamlet* and *Romeo and Juliet* given by a visiting English company in Paris. He later calls this 'the supreme drama of my life'. In a brain-altering two-way tackle Shakespeare reveals the true nature of Art, while Irish actress Harriet Smithson (2), playing both Ophelia and Juliet, has him instantly smitten. After *Romeo*, Berlioz allegedly leaves the theatre saying 'I will marry that woman and write my greatest symphony on the play.' Good copy, but untrue. In the end, though, Berlioz does both.

SWOONING

1827–1830   His obsession with Harriet takes on epic proportions. Berlioz behaves erratically, boring his friends. His stage door Johnny antics terrify the Irishwoman who warns others to 'beware the gentleman with the strange eyes'.

1830   Berlioz hears rumours that Harriet is sleeping with her manager. After emotional tempest and numerous long walks he writes the *Fantastic Symphony* in six weeks. He then falls for eighteen-year-old pianist Camille Moke (3). Requited lust is a big factor here. They become engaged. Berlioz reluctantly leaves for Italy after winning a prestigious composition prize. The lovers exchange rings and make vows of eternal constancy.

1831   Berlioz is told that Camille is to marry a rich piano manufacturer. He leaves for Paris with plans to shoot the faithless pair, plus her mother, and then kill himself while dressed in drag. He loses his frocks and resolve when his baggage goes missing en route. Change of plan: he jumps off a cliff into the sea. Splashing down near a fishing boat, he is conveniently rescued. Chastened, he writes a sequel to the *Fantastic Symphony* celebrating his return to life. He calls it *Lélio, or The Return to Life*.

1832   Berlioz returns to Paris from Italy and discovers that Harriet is also back in town. He rents a room formerly occupied by the actress. Passion reawakens. The *Fantastic Symphony* and *Lélio* are performed at a concert in December. The Symphony's printed programme – the descriptions attached to the music – tells of a young man who overdoses because of unrequited love, but misjudges the dosage and instead experiences a series of nightmares in which she is always present: the whirl of a ball, the isolation of the countryside, being driven to his own execution, and her transformation into a hag at a witches' Sabbath. The 'beloved' in question is represented by a recurring theme – a 'fixed idea', or *idée fixe* – that all present in the audience know to be the emblem of Harriet herself. She attends the concert and is the subject of great attention. Afterwards she and Berlioz are formally introduced. One week later, they declare their love for each other.

1833 Harriet becomes Mrs Berlioz after a campaign of resistance from the composer's family. She is, after all, poor, Protestant, and an actress with a history.

1839 As allegedly pledged, Berlioz composes his *Romeo and Juliet* Symphony.

1842 Marie Recio (4), a dark-eyed but untalented singer, becomes Berlioz's mistress. Harriet begins to slide into alcohol-fuddled despair.

1844   The Berlioz ménage finally splinters; the 'supreme drama' of his life is over. Marie is now his constant companion.

1854   Harriet dies after a series of strokes. Liszt writes a letter of consolation to Berlioz saying 'she inspired you, you loved her, you sang of her, her task was done'. Berlioz marries Marie Recio.

1862   Marie Recio dies suddenly from a heart attack. Berlioz falls in love with a mysterious woman less than half his age called Amélie (5).

1864   Berlioz literally stumbles across Amélie's grave in the Montmartre cemetery. This is something of an unpleasant surprise, as you can imagine. Harriet's remains need to be relocated to make room for a new street in the modernisation of Paris and Berlioz witnesses her disinterment. Hamlet-like, he contemplates the now-detached head of his Ophelia/Juliet.

1864–1865   Berlioz decides to go back to No 1 and resumes contact with Estelle, now in her late sixties. But the loop does not fully close. While he is finally able to declare his affection, she tells him to cool off because she's now too old for that sort of thing. Berlioz resigns himself to adoring her from afar, calling her his 'distant star'.

It is a sad story. A man who gave his life to music and love felt at the end, with good cause, that he had been unsuccessful in both. And yet he could still write the quote at the beginning of this chapter, saying in addition:

'Love and Music are the two wings of the soul.'

~

Love Kills

'All of a sudden, my heart sings' says the popular song from the 1950s, and I can think of no better reason for the invention of opera in Italy in the late sixteenth century. In *Orfeo* (1607) by Claudio Monteverdi, the earliest opera to be still performed regularly, the eponymous musician of antiquity is widowed and vents his grief so persuasively that at least one sentimental old god decides that Orpheus can nip down to the netherworld, collect his wife and keep going as if nothing has happened. There is one string attached; he must avert his eyes from her during the return journey. In opera, everyone is too dim to honour any sort of pact (a convention established for the new genre by plotlines such as this) and Orpheus sneaks a look. His wife drops dead, again. Orpheus promptly resumes whingeing and grieving. The gods, moved yet another time and no doubt anxious to shut Orpheus up once and for all, bring Eurydice back to life and reunite the pair.

Love conquers all in opera – even death itself, at times. Still, even the divine Monteverdi allowed sex to drive the plot by the end of his career. In his final opera *The Coronation of Poppea* (1642), a story of top-level hijinks in ancient Rome, the Emperor Nero casts aside his wife for a manipulative superior bonk. Not only do the baddies succeed and get away with it, they serenade their triumph in one of the most beautiful love duets ever written.

Opera is a dangerous place. High voices spend half the night tasting the pleasures of love only to find themselves dead by the end of the show. Forget about the supposedly ennobling aspects of high art; in the hands of someone like Giacomo Puccini (1858–1924) the tunes are fabulous, but those gals are going down.

Serial Soprano Killer: A Case History

Manon Lescaut (1893)

Soprano: Manon, a young girl.
Turpitude: Inflames the heart of student Des Grieux. They decamp. Des Grieux runs dry of cash. Manon becomes the mistress of a treasurer-general,* accepting jewels and frocks as compensation for older flesh. Continues to consort with

Des Grieux and tells treasurer-general she likes it this way.
Consequence paid: Manon dragged to jail as a thief. Eventually she is deported to Louisiana with a shipload of loose women.
Death: Dehydration, depression and exhaustion on a New Orleans plain.

*Note: Opera tends to stereotype politicians as middle-aged or older, wealthy, emotionally dysfunctional and manipulative. In return, politicians make the same accusations about opera.

La Bohème (1896)

Soprano: Mimi, a seamstress.
Turpitude: Pops into garret of impoverished poet Rodolfo looking for a light. Fifteen minutes, two arias and a duet later, they are in love and Mimi is odds on to stay the night after a quick drink on the town. They move in together somewhere between Acts Two and Three.
Consequence paid: Ménage of emotional hell exacerbated by Rodolfo's concern for her health. Tearful separation. Mimi becomes the mistress of someone with more money.
Death: Tuberculosis. That nasty cough from Act One finally catches up with her.

Tosca (1900)

Soprano: Floria Tosca, fragrant diva in a sea of political intrigue.

Turpitude: Nuts about artistic type Cavaradossi, who is friend and abetter of revolutionaries. He is captured by evil Scarpia, the Chief of Police, and interrogated under torture while Tosca watches. She agrees to Scarpia's terms of Cavaradossi's freedom in exchange for sexual favours. As the Chief prepares to lower the britches, she stabs him to death with the famous line 'this is Tosca's kiss'.*

Consequence paid: What was to have been a mock execution of Cavaradossi by firing squad turns horribly real. Tosca ends up with a dead lover.

Death: Suicide, throwing herself from the top of a castle. Unlike the standard operatic death scene, Tosca does not sing on the way down.

Note: Even real-life opera singers are given to extremes. See future chapters.

Madama Butterfly (1904)

Soprano: Cio-Cio-San (Butterfly), fifteen-year-old Japanese contract bride.

Turpitude: None, since she is an innocent and honourable girl who sticks to her contract. Taken as bride by visiting US Navy lieutenant Pinkerton, who certainly sounds sincere in the concluding Act One duet. She conceives and gives birth during the intermission, during which Pinkerton, ducking out for a loaf of bread, disappears for three years and takes a legitimate wife back in the States. Somewhat insensitively, the American couple find

themselves back at Butterfly's place in Nagasaki.
Consequence paid: Love and honour betrayed, Butterfly realises she was part of a lousy contract.
Death: Harakiri.

Suor Angelica (1918)

Soprano: Suor Angelica (Sister Angelica), a nun.
Turpitude: Unmarried mother. Not a good look in seventeenth-century Florentine aristocracy.
Consequence paid: Forced into nunnery and separated from child. She is later told by a disapproving aunt of the child's death.
Death: Suicide by home-brew poison. Audience begins to wonder when Puccini will give the soprano a break.

Turandot (1924)

Soprano: Liù, a young Chinese slave girl.
Turpitude: Not having the title role, which has been taken by another soprano, who is presumably collecting a bigger fee. Nevertheless, she loves the tenor.
Consequence paid: Consigned to pitiable 'girl next door' role; clearly will not get the tenor.
Death: Puccini's, leaving Act Three unfinished after having Liù commit suicide. The sopranos' karmic revenge.

Serenades

Opera deaths are larger than life – or larger than death. For the real-life lover (as opposed to the fictional character onstage) something more intimate is required. Hence the serenade with its classic image of a besotted fellow in tights crooning up to the balcony of his girlfriend's room in the middle of a summer night – without waking the neighbours. The nocturnal *al fresco* confession of love was certainly popular by the late sixteenth century, if Shakespeare's *Romeo and Juliet* is any indication; the musical version was described in a German lexicon of 1732. The word itself derives from the Latin *serenus*, and one imagines that someone in southern Europe thought of it first during a hot night.

Eventually the serenade became a much bigger deal, involving lots of instruments and more extended forms. The neighbours would have been furious, but by then balconies and girlfriends had been taken out of the equation. Mozart wrote serenades for wind instruments (including his *Gran Partita* with its divine Adagio movement) and Brahms put in some early symphonic practice with a couple of serenades for orchestra.

If you are a courageous, mellow-voiced reader, keen on outdoor sports, you might like to consider the revitalisation of the serenade. I must say that in my experience I've never heard it done successfully, but this could be due to a bad choice of music. The classical composers provide serenades by the truckload: Mozart in several operas (*Don Giovanni*, *The Abduction from the Seraglio*, *Così fan tutte*), Rossini and Donizetti likewise, while the cosier genre of art song or the parlour ballad is littered with very singable efforts by Schubert, Tosti and Mascagni. Really, many song composers have bequeathed to us a romantic ditty or two worth having a crack at with a guitar. Of course, if your beloved lives above the second floor you may have to resort to singing into a mobile phone. It doesn't carry quite the same theatrical impact to have Don Giovanni emailing a sound file.

One serenades with an ulterior motive: an invitation up to the balcony via the nearest trellis for a cup of chamomile tea, perhaps, or a quick retune of the lute for a face-to-face duet in close harmony. In the Middle Ages, around the twelfth and thirteenth centuries, the French troubadours and trouvères went for more of a no-strings-attached model. They sang of courtly love (or as they called it in their time, *fin'amor*) which was more of a 'look, love, but don't touch' non-affair. To touch would not only have been a vulgar capitulation to sensual desire, but a breach of protocol; troubadours were supposed to love women above their station. Sometimes they would love them without actually having seen them. When at last they set eyes on their ideal, they then swooned themselves into an early grave. It seems a little counter-productive.

A troubadour's love was expressed purely by the highest courtesy and a rich repertoire of poetry and song, some of the greatest of the time. And there were hundreds of these fellows wandering around the courts of Europe, loitering behind columns and sublimating their love-sickness with a song every time they caught a passing whiff of rose petals. It is amazing there were enough unattainable women to go around. Fragrant longing was the style; one only maintained a presence in those exalted corridors by being 'courteous and accomplished'.

Love songs went on to become some of the biggest hits of their time. Frenchman Claudin de Sermisy (1490–1562) scored during the Renaissance with his chanson *Tant que vivray*, which translates 'to As long as I live in my prime, I shall serve the mighty king of Love'. This was arranged for all sorts of vocal and instrumental combinations and appeared in publications right through until 1644. A hundred years at Number One – it wouldn't happen these days.

Essential Love Aids

The following have proved instrumental in the exercise of music for lovers.

LOVE

The flute

The soft complaining flute
In dying notes discovers
The woes of hopeless lovers . . .
John Dryden, *A Song for St Cecilia's Day* (1687)

The cello

The cello is like a beautiful woman who has not grown older, but younger with time, more slender, more supple, more graceful.
Pablo Casals*, TIME magazine (1957)

**Casals knew what he was talking about. When he married for the second time, he was decades older than his new father-in-law. Quizzed about the physical dangers of taking a bride sixty years his junior, Casals said 'I look at it this way: if she dies, she dies.'*

The viola d'amore

These days, the members of the violin family heard in symphony orchestras tout only four strings apiece, but this voluptuary with a whiff of the Middle East about her sound has no fewer than fourteen: seven playing strings and another seven underneath which resonate with sympathetic vibrations. A gentle swipe of the bow and you achieve sonic coercion. There is also an oboe *d'amore* in the woodwind family, but in this case the name refers to the sound of the instrument rather than the means of its production. What a lost opportunity; surely a wind instrument requiring *two* sets of lips for its operation would have been more popular.

Some Useful Love Advice

1. Take care with actresses:

Classical music suggests that you marry a thespian at your peril. Hector Berlioz and Harriet are explained in sorry detail above.

» Richard Wagner's first marriage to Minna Planer had a rocky start and only spluttered back to life when he or she wasn't involved with someone else at the time (see *Triumph*).

» The conductor Leopold Stokowski enjoyed a much-publicised liaison with Greta Garbo in the 1930s, fuelled mainly by his curiosity about making love to a lesbian. He later said it was wonderful.

» In the 1902 opera *Adriana Lecouvreur* by Cilea we have a Count and a Prince in love with duelling actresses. Adriana herself eventually succumbs to the fatal scent of poisoned violets sent by her rival. They really can be so nasty to each other.

2. Singers are a better bet:

One would have thought a diva to be dangerous, but there is evident domestic happiness to be had with a soprano.

» Classical music's perfect match could well have been that of Norwegian composer Edvard Grieg (1843–1907) and his wife (and first cousin) Nina. They married young and remained blissfully happy and serene for the next forty years. He wrote songs for her; she sang them at their joint recitals. Just a few years before he predeceased her Grieg wrote 'once in my life I was touched with genius. The genius was Love'.

» Opera composers were likewise attracted to the singing incarnations of their muse: Verdi's second wife and Rossini's first were loving and long-term companions. The German Richard Strauss (1864–1949) married soprano Pauline de Ahna in 1894 and presented four of his best songs to her as a wedding gift. She wore the pants at home; Strauss once confessed to Mahler 'My wife's a bit rough, but that's what I need'.

» Closer to our own time, the relationship between Benjamin Britten (1913–1976) and tenor Peter

Pears was the inspiration of some of the greatest vocal and operatic music of the twentieth century.

3. Go back for seconds (or more):
Love can indeed be lovelier with a rerun.

» Johann Sebastian Bach (1685–1750) enjoyed a happy and fruitful marriage to his second cousin, Maria Barbara, until her early death in 1720, leaving Johann with a few little Bachs to feed. (He was an enthusiastic and tireless baby-maker.) Wife Number Two was twenty-year-old Anna Magdalena, sixteen years younger than the composer, who was obviously going to match him baby for baby. They started with a new one each year, eventually relaxing the pace a little as Bach moved into his mid-fifties; although the mortality rate was high (the norm for the early eighteenth century) at any given time there would have been ten children running around the house. The dutiful Anna Magdalena even kept a hand-written music-book for the kiddies' studies. Many of the Bach boys became composers.

» Likewise Verdi, Shostakovich, Rossini, Stravinsky and Wagner enjoyed great luck at the second attempt after being widowed, even though the last two were merely marrying their long-time mistresses. Wagner began to fall in love with his second wife Cosima when she accepted his offer of a lift back to a hotel in an empty wheelbarrow.

» Mozart was rejected by Aloysia Weber (a singer!) before working his way down the line to fall in love and marry her younger sister Constanze. A good, lustful marriage replete with penis jokes ensued (see *Lust*).

» The itinerant piano virtuoso and composer Henry Litolff (1818–1891) was enthusiastic about marriage, but not a great stayer. Early keenness was shown in his elopement at the age of seventeen with his soon-to-be first wife who was a year younger. They separated soon after, but his attempts over the next few years to secure a divorce were unsuccessful; one of them resulting in a heavy fine and a spell in an English prison, from which he escaped after sweet-talking one of the warden's wives. Two more marriages and divorces followed. Finally, in his late fifties, he took as his fourth wife a seventeen-year-old girl who had been his nurse during a period of illness. She continued in this role for his remaining fifteen years.

4. *A note for wives:*

Á propos to the above, remember this – he may look interesting and display an attractively mercurial temperament now, but you could be in for trouble further down the track.

» Robert Schumann (1810–1856) and his wife Clara Wieck were married after what is possibly the most famous and dramatic romance in music: she, the brilliant and wilful daughter of Schumann's piano teacher; he, a bundle of nervous energy that bordered on the manic. Clara was a teenage piano prodigy; Robert was a promising player whose ambitions were foiled abruptly after he maimed a finger on his right hand with a bizarre contraption he'd invented to help him with his practice. Clara's dad did all he could to poison the liaison with letters, slanders and legal proceedings. Love triumphed and they married the day before Clara's twenty-first birthday in September 1840. Their bliss was punctuated by Robert's depressions and breakdowns. In 1854 he threw himself into the Rhine after speaking of the taunting voices of devils interrupting his sleep. He spent the next two-and-a-half years in an asylum without seeing his wife or children. They set eyes on each other only the day before he died, probably of self-starvation.

» Jelka Rosen, the wife of Frederick Delius (1862–1934) was also taking on a handful, given that he had long been infected with syphilis when they married in 1903. Twenty years later he was blind, paralysed and confined to a wheelchair. The strain of his care must have been immense; although she never contracted the disease from her husband, Jelka's health declined almost as fast. She died less than a year after him.

A Final Word

We come back to Berlioz, whose attitude to romance in his middle age had changed from the ardour of his *Fantastic Symphony*. In the final song of his cycle about love, called *Summer Nights* (*Les nuits d'été*), a traveller asks to be taken to the place where love lasts forever. 'Alas', says the boatman, 'no such place exists'.

∽

For the sake of this book's premise, we'll assume that the relationship has enjoyed this glorious start. From such uncomplicated matters of the heart, the music now takes us downward to a darker mood – and another part of the anatomy.

Lust

*'I slept with that woman for seven years.
Wouldn't you think she'd remember that I hate fish?'*
Arturo Toscanini
to a friend after being served caviar
by a former mistress

The history of music is a hormonal one. Lust looms large in the success or failure of musical careers, the psychology of performers and composers, and (according to some) the very contours of music itself. Sex in classical music has confused the censors and outraged audiences – when they weren't being stimulated. Morals have been affronted; bosoms set heaving. Music of great attractiveness is described as 'ravishing', as if it were a passionate lover.

We don't need a central composer figure in *Lust*, unlike the other chapters, because, let's face it, everyone was doing it. Sexually transmitted diseases darkened or ended the lives of the greats (Schumann, Chabrier, Donizetti, Schubert and Delius, to name a few). Bach's twenty-plus children and Mozart's explicit letters to his wife are proof of their vigorous marriages. Many other musicians shopped around. For performers, then as now, it was a life 'on the road'. Liszt was popular for more than merely flashing a mean arpeggio. One of Liszt's illegitimate daughters pursued a long adulterous relationship with Wagner, bearing him three children before their eventual marriage.

In the turbulent world of opera, coitus is usually attempted before intermission, and never more so than with Mozart, writing for the supposedly genteel audiences of eighteenth-century Vienna. At the very beginning of *The Marriage of Figaro* the eponymous hero is seen measuring up the space available for the essential item of the nuptial bed. *Don Giovanni*, like *Figaro*, is set to a libretto by the seemingly priapic Lorenzo da Ponte, whose good friend Giacomo Casanova appears to have functioned here as a sort of script consultant.

At which point we might pause for:

A Message To The Gentlemen Readers:

> **MEN!**
> *Ever find the discipline of monogamy too burdensome? Do the exploits of a Don Juan or a Casanova make you just a little envious?*

If so, you'll find a vicarious pleasure in Mozart's 1787 opera *Don Giovanni*. The Don is a Spanish nobleman who simply cannot have enough women. And when the persuasion of rank is not enough, force will have to do. He commits a rape and a murder in the first five minutes, but becomes more charming as time goes on. Or perhaps he just seems to, as the master psychologist Mozart drags us down to the Don's level. Certainly there is plenty of ringside action as we watch him with three women on the trot and a fourth in his sights in Act Two.

We discover his rate of conquest through the statistics offered by the Don's servant Leporello in the famous 'Catalogue' Aria. Notches in the bedhead would have turned his furniture to woodchips, so Leporello makes entries in a ledger according to nationality. It includes 640 Italian *bellas,* 231 German *Fräuleins*, 100 French *mesdames*, a rather lacklustre 91 Turks, and in his home hunting ground of Spain 1,003 and counting (there is something gruesomely comic about this number just edging into four figures). The aria profiles the pathology and the technique of the sexual compulsive: fair-haired women are praised for their kindliness, brunettes for their constancy, and blondes for their sweetness. The Don calls tall women 'majestic' and short women 'dainty'. His indiscriminate tastes make him very PC. Every age, shape and social class is fair game; for instance, plump women are preferred during the colder months. This is 1787 and electric blankets are a long way off.

Observe the date and marvel at Mozart's prescience. The French Revolution and the beginning of the end of the aristocracy is just around the corner, crowds roaring in triumph as uncomprehending and unrepentant nobility met the guillotine. Mozart uses the Don's rampant genitals as a symbol of all that is wrong with his world; at least, that is what I suspect he's doing. It would be a pity if a sexual enthusiast like Mozart was going a little prudish on us by suggesting that all dashing ladies' men with too much petrol in the tank go to Hell. For that is the fate that befalls Don Giovanni at the end of the opera.

∼

Mozart himself was nothing like the Don: as a musician, in his time he was considered nothing more than a servant, and frequently short of cash – but not as destitute as legend would have it. While not promiscuous, he was certainly not an abstainer, and it is refreshing to read of his continuing lust for his wife Constanze. As he wrote to his father, 'her whole beauty consists of two little black eyes and a beautiful figure'. Constanze was a nice, kind girl who happened to turn Wolfgang on. He was twenty-five and frisky. So was she; the engagement almost fell apart when she allowed a strange man to measure her calves during a party game. Mozart claimed first dibs on her calves and the rest of the ensemble, telling her in his letters on tour of his longing for her backside and for her 'dear little nest', a receptacle for his 'little boy', which, even as he writes (in 1789) 'sneaks onto the table and looks at me enquiringly'. This has nothing to do whatsoever with his subsequent opera *The Magic Flute*.

Sixteen years after Mozart's death, *Don Giovanni's* Danish premiere featured the Swiss-born Éduoard Du Puy, also a composer, in the title role. He seems to have taken the part to heart. When later employed at the Royal Court to teach singing to the Princess consort of Prince Christian Frederik – later Christian VIII – the pupil ill-advisedly fell in love with her teacher. Both were exiled, ending his career in that country.

The last of the Mozart–Da Ponte collaborations, *Così fan tutte* (1789) is an exploration of sexual morality. Two sisters are engaged to officers who make a wager with a cynical old bachelor about their fiancées' fidelity. The younger men trust their partners, while the bachelor maintains that in the right conditions morality takes a back seat; as he says, 'Così fan tutte' (all women behave like this).

So how quickly can morals be subverted and the obligations of fidelity be swamped by a surfeit of suggestions in foreign accents and a set of tanned loins? And if our bleary-eyed guinea pigs do stray, what does that say about the shallowness and sexual opportunism of society in Mozart's day, and ours?

A set-up is staged wherein the officers are suddenly called off to war, only to be supplanted by the equally abrupt appearance of two swarthy Albanians who are, of course, the same officers in turbans with a little boot polish on their faces. They begin to chat up the other's girlfriend, and this partner-swapping exercise pays off within the day when wedding plans are announced after heavy petting and marvellous ensemble singing.

So much for the good old days; we should never believe the cant about a 'purer' age put about by parents and self-appointed moralists. Mozart reminds us that human impulse and our incapacity to control it all the time hasn't changed for hundreds of years. The remedy? A good laugh, and an acceptance of our predictable fallibility, much as the characters do at the opera's conclusion.

More Sex, Please

Aldous Huxley once quoted an Italian proverb: 'Bed is the poor man's opera'. One could invert the phrase and say with confidence that opera has been the rich man's bed. Opera plots are full of rich, powerful older men coveting sexual favours from younger women, but there are also innumerable operas in which those women use intelligence and guile to turn the situation to their advantage.

In Puccini's *Tosca*, alluded to earlier, the beautiful singer knows that the chief of police Baron Scarpia wants more than just her arias, and allows him to think he has won before administering her deadly 'kiss'. The nubile Salome in Richard Strauss' 1905 opera is quite prepared to drop all seven of her veils for the sexually demented Herod in exchange for the real object of her desire. That this turns out to be John the Baptist's severed head explains why opera is best enjoyed after dinner.

The *femme fatale* of Alban Berg's 1937 *Lulu* is on the wrong end of sexual revenge when she encounters Jack the Ripper at the end of the show. Two centuries before this, the maid Serpina ('little snake' in Italian) tricks her way into marrying her wealthy and elderly employer Uberto in the one-act comedy *La serva padrona*, or 'The Maid as Mistress' (1736). Long before the French Revolution, using sex appeal as a blunt instrument was a justifiable exit strategy for women trapped by gender and social caste. Once liberated, women could be more selective. The Scottish-American soprano Mary Garden (1874–1967) stirred many a male opera fan's loins, being unusually svelte by diva standards of the day. An elderly admirer, staring at her décolletage, asked what kept her strapless dress up.

'Your age, sir,' she replied.

There was room for bestiality in opera plots as well. In Darius Milhaud's 1927 mini-opera *The Rape of Europa* the aforementioned Europa ends her relationship with Pergamon upon discovering her love of animals. He is, understandably, furious.

Sex? Really?

Today's countertenors trilling the vocal acrobatics written for the *castrati* of the Baroque are in vogue – but (much to their relief) they are not the real thing. The original male glamour singers were much sought after by the leading composers of opera and the subject of adulation by audiences. Their voices soared with the almost unearthly purity of a boy soprano because that is effectively what they were, their pre-pubescent range having been retained thanks to surgical intervention. A quick nip here and there, two faint plops in a jar, and one was high for life, the boyish notes amplified by a grown man's frame.

The most famous castrato of all was Farinelli (1705–1782). (Stars of this magnitude often sported single stage names, rather like today's fashion designers, hypnotists or Madonna.) Offstage, his non-vocal displays would also surprise those who thought that with a couple of jacks removed from the deck, offering a full house was impossible. This was understandable: how often have you talked with a eunuch about virility? In fact, the *castrati* could delight their more ardent admirers with all the confidence of a walking contraceptive.

The vigorous Caffarelli (aka Gaetano Majorano, 1710–1783) certainly did. He was one of Europe's favourites, serenading French dauphines through the latter stages of their pregnancies, and premiering the title role in George Frideric Handel's opera *Serse* (*Xerxes*, 1738), with the famous aria composed expressly for him, *Ombra mai fu*, a touching sentiment addressed to a tree. The virtuoso singer once shared a stage with a live elephant and several camels, upstaging all of them.

Caffarelli's was the true prima donna temperament. He was thrown in prison in 1741 for making indecent gestures at the audience during a performance, and had earlier been under house arrest after attacking a colleague in a Naples church while a nun was taking the veil. For certain female admirers of his voice he was happy to offer proof of the knife-hewn pudding. In Rome in 1728 he was surprised *in flagrante* by a returning husband and had to spend the rest of the night hiding in a disused water tank. Anxious that he not go the way of a Stradella (see below), Caffarelli's mistress hired bodyguards to protect the singer from her husband's revenge for the rest of his stay.

A hundred years later, with the *castrati* a distant memory on the opera stage, a different type of sex god bestrode the new arena of the concert hall: pianist Franz Liszt (1811–1886). When the exotic, longhaired Hungarian played in Berlin in 1842, the audience went bananas. Adoring women collected the broken strings from the pianos at the end of his recitals and had them converted into bracelets. Other cast-offs also became souvenirs: coffee dregs were preserved in perfume bottles, and cigar butts were lovingly hidden in cleavages. The term 'Lisztomania' was invented to describe the phenomenon.

And if you thought that refuge from this constant worldly, erotic clamour could be found in the local monastery – forget it. The outpourings of randy and dipsomaniacal medieval monks are captured in *Carmina Burana*, set to music by the German Carl Orff in 1935–1936. Its opening chorus, *O Fortuna*, is one of classical music's most identifiable anthems because of its frequent use in television commercials and movie trailers; there's a wild, almost heathen nature to its surging chant about the capriciousness of Fate – the mob speaks. Early on the text expresses a desire to lie in the arms of the Queen of England. This is well before the Elizabeths, of course.

Did Someone Mention In Flagrante?

Sex killed Alessandro Stradella (1644–1682), one of the most famous Italian composers of his time, but disease or exhaustion were not factors in his demise. He paid the ultimate price for repeatedly ignoring a maxim that holds true to this day: don't filch your employer's merchandise.

Stradella first hit trouble in his native Rome in 1669 when he tried to embezzle money from the Roman Catholic Church in company with a corrupt abbot and a violinist. In the ensuing scandal the young composer left town. It was the first of several quick exits.

One such scamper to Venice dropped Stradella in it even further. A member of a powerful local family, one Alvise Contarini, decided his mistress should study music and hired Stradella for the job. Music soon proved the food of something else, and Stradella decamped with his pupil. Never cross a Venetian; the outraged Contarini gathered forty henchmen and tracked the traitorous music teacher to Turin, bent on vengeance.

Stradella was saved by the diplomatic protection of a friendly local regent, but Contarini slipped some *scudi* to two more assassins, who made an attempt on the composer's life in October 1677. Legend has it that they were going to ambush him after a concert of his music in Rome, but finding his work so much to their taste they instead introduced themselves, complimented Stradella on his gorgeous oratorio and advised him to get the hell out of there. What a sentimental old pair of back-stabbers. You don't find too many hired killers with a refined aesthetic sense these days.

Stradella's brains stayed firmly in his britches, even after such warnings. In early 1682 in Genoa he was at it again, this time with a young woman 'connected' with the Lomellini family. This was the final straw. The soldier who was set upon him was obviously less partial to sonatas; the errant composer was stabbed to death in a piazza.

A more immediate post-coital death was inflicted upon the wife of the slightly mad and exceedingly angry Prince of Venosa, Don Carlo Gesualdo (1561–1613). She had been amusing herself with the Duke of Andria, unaware that her husband had got wind of the affair. It would seem that seventeenth-century Italians didn't handle this sort of thing very well. One evening when Mrs G and her cavalier were savouring the proverbial cigarette, secure in the belief that Don Carlo was away inspecting his estates, the seething Prince burst into the bedroom armed with a gun and a stiletto knife. The former he emptied into the Duke, while the latter was employed on his wife in a precursor to the shower scene from *Psycho*. He eventually tired of murdering and became a composer of madrigals that still sound weird today.

SEX ON LEGS

Ah, the waltz – that respectable incarnation of the romance and style of old Vienna! That is how we think of it these days. But the whirling dance in triple time involving close contact broke through the strangulated body language of early nineteenth-century Europe like an obscene gesture. The advent of the waltz in England in around 1812 inspired the press to liken it to copulation. A general and a young fop fought a duel over its acceptability; shots were fired, but bodies, souls and feet were spared. At last, society could enjoy an acceptable choreographic grope. In an uncharacteristic gesture of prudery Lord Byron, published an anti-waltz poem under a pseudonym:

Hot from the hands promiscuously applied,
Round the slight waist, or down the glowing side

The breast thus publicly resigned to man
In private may resist him – if it can.

Horace Hornem, Esq,

The Waltz: An Apostrophic Hymn (1813)

Sex In Music

Just what is all the fuss about Ravel's *Bolero*? Even before Dudley Moore and Bo Derek used it as a lovemaking aid in the 1979 film *10* the work had somehow earned a reputation as classical music's ultimate aphrodisiac. But with that film's success the *Bolero*'s erotic power became legend and every self-respecting Lothario kept a recording along with the incense and the mirror over the bed.

Written as a ballet score in 1928 for Ravel's friend Ida Rubinstein and her ballet troupe, the original scenario does carry a strong undercurrent of sex: a young woman dancing alone in a dim Spanish café to an audience of men. Since then the piece has made its way onto the concert platform, creating its own sensual aroma without the help of pictures. It began getting under people's skins almost immediately; even during Ravel's lifetime it was used in a 1934 Paramount film called *Bolero*, which starred Carole Lombard and George Raft.

We're often told that artists create from direct experience.

In this instance it is difficult to associate the sinuous and apparently orgasmic writhing of the *Bolero* with the persona of its composer. Ravel, in short, was not a raver. We simply don't know if this diminutive, secretive dandy ever spoiled the perfect creases in his trousers by lowering them for anybody.

His own description of the work is hardly erotic: 'seventeen minutes of orchestration without music', he wrote; 'an experiment in a special and limited direction'. If this sounds like a description of a score in handcuffs, one has to acknowledge that there *is* a whiff of bondage about it: one tune, one rhythm and no development. The basic materials are bound, gagged and tortured in Chinese-water style by the ceaseless tapping of a snare drum. Each time that unchanging tune comes around there are a few more instruments involved, making one long crescendo. The thrust is the same; only the equipment gets bigger. Finally, the harmony explodes into another key but the ropes stay on – nobody is going to stop that bloody drum. A couple more bangs and it's over. Where, I ask you, was the foreplay? Couldn't they have tried another position (key signature)? That's it – seventeen minutes? Most importantly, why doesn't Ravel offer us a cigarette?

This is not to disparage the *Bolero*'s undeniable impact. Like any talented lover it almost demands a standing ovation after each performance. But as in most of the meanings we 'perceive' in music, its sexual allure is our own collective projection from the less-frequented parts of our erotic natures. Ravel's music was criticised in his time for being 'reptilian' and 'cold-blooded'. It seems that some of us like the idea of a one-night stand with a stranger in snakeskin.

Many years ago I was producing a recording of the *Bolero* for the Sydney Symphony Orchestra. The conductor, Stuart Challender, noted with some amusement that our recording date was St Valentine's Day. We all put in a hard morning's work re-recording 'patches' of the piece before our final take: number 69.

~

Imputing erotic meaning to the *Bolero* is wasteful when many other composers are happy to provide more explicit commentary. In Claude Debussy's *Prelude to the Afternoon of a Faun* (1894) our cloven-footed hero is cavorting with a bevy of naked nymphs (according to Stéphane Mallarmé's original poem). Or is he just dreaming about it? That's the faun's flute at the start, by the way.

Scriabin's *The Poem of Ecstasy* (1908) evokes copulation on a cosmic scale, describing the union of the 'male Creator-Spirit and the Woman-World'. The orchestra is appropriately huge for this heavyweight encounter, with a solo trumpet in the lead role of the Phallus. This is the only orchestral piece I know about multiple orgasms; then again, I could be just dreaming about it. Scriabin originally called it 'The Orgiastic Poem'.

For a terrific musical orgy you can do no better than the final Bacchanale of the ballet *Daphnis and Chloé* (1912), by (here he is again) Ravel. The story is simple: boy meets girl, girl abducted by pirates, pirates frightened by an apparition of the god Pan, girl and boy reunited and all celebrate. Listen to the chorus as they whoop and pant in rhythm over the whirring orchestra. Don't tell me they're just playing cards. For me this supple and voluptuous score leaves *Bolero* in the shade for sex appeal.

Back on the home playing field, one can't overlook Richard Strauss' *Domestic Symphony* (1903), a portrait of the pleasures to be had with the family. According to the programme, or written narrative illustrated by the music, Strauss has had a pleasant evening playing with his child. The clock strikes seven and the composer and his wife retire. A 'Love Scene' ensues with a highly evocative series of musical gestures, before the clock strikes seven the next morning. The listener need apply only a small amount of imagination.

It is *such* a relief to learn of such ribaldry in people whom we esteem. All those juices have to go somewhere, and it would be a shock if the tip of the quill alone proved a sufficiently wide conduit. We try too hard to perceive composers as fleshless puritans. Strangely, we've never expected artists or writers to be such cleanskins, and it is the rock performers of today who have staked out the 'bad boy' territory in music. A modern painter is somehow more credible if he is flouting the law or battling an addiction ('she' should be more controlled – another stereotype), whereas we still attach just a bit of the same old livery to modern composers that Mozart rebelled against in 1781. We will souvenir postcards of the nudes in any gallery shop but be rather more circumspect about asking for a copy of Francis Poulenc's 1944 opera *The Breasts of Tiresias* (great piece, by the way). Which brings us to ...

Sex Sells?

Recent discussion of the 'crisis' in classical music reveals the pomposity that always attaches to any discussion of so-called 'high' and 'low' art. We don't really know what distinguishes the two; nevertheless we become extremely upset if we suspect they've been mixed together.

The great composers occupy lofty positions in our pantheon of Western achievement. Nothing gets much 'higher'. But they're not unassailable, it seems; some of those lily-white countenances have begun to bear the dirty fingerprints of the rapacious marketeers. That, at least, is the chorus of complaint from some anxious cultural observers.

It goes something like this: in an orgy of profit-mongering and desecration, poor Mozart and Beethoven have been allowed to consort with pouting hussies and toy boys, who occasionally let their appearance get in the way of a good performance. Entire symphonies and concertos have been carved up by CD compilations and certain radio stations, and the bleeding chunks offered to a public newly wracked by short concentration spans for ease of consumption. Dear old Father Bach, who spent a productive lifetime writing music 'for the glory of God', now provides mere accompaniment to the more mundane glories of cocktail tippling, supermarket browsing and perhaps even the odd naughty.

Even the CD *Swoon* compilations that preceded this book caused murmurs of discontent. If almost everyone was buying them, it stood to reason that I had vulgarised this wonderful material by some dreadful lowbrow approach: a single-word description, a 'brand', trivialising the music by stealing away its indefinable, non-verbal message and complexity of approach. It blandly dictated to the listener how you should respond, and if you were gullible enough to follow, you were not the sort of person who should be listening to the stuff in the first place. You and I were therefore complicit in a vast public idiocy.

In these desperate days of imploding CD sales, record-company marketing receives short shrift from wowsers who complain that talent is now subordinate to looks, worthiness to expediency and a fast buck. The young are in. One should always be suspicious of people who whinge about an increasing predilection for youth; it usually means that the complainant is simply getting older. There *is* a wave of, say, young female violinists who look appealing on CD covers, and they can all certainly play a mean fiddle. Jascha Heifetz played a mean fiddle too, but he theoretically wouldn't get a look-in today unless he looked as fetching as Anne-Sophie Mutter in a strapless dress.

Of course there have been some deliberate attempts to make sales through titillation. Vanessa-Mae posed for covers in wet T-shirts, and has sold well too (not, I suspect, by dragging potential buyers away from Jascha Heifetz). Linda Brava generated some publicity by appearing only with her violin in *Playboy* magazine. Men are also caught up in this; it has not escaped public notice that tenor Jonas Kaufmann is better looking than Enrico Caruso. (We are also aware that he is a fabulous singer.) Conductors need extravagant hair, singers require *haute couture* and makeovers, record shelves are crowded with come-hither expressions – titillation has been let loose in classical music's sacred precincts.

The only thing new in classical music is this puritanism. If there is one thing you'll have learned from this chapter, it is that sex has been present in classical music all along. I doubt this brutal discovery means that you love the music any less; in fact, your understanding of it can only increase. It would be perverse if such a vital element of life were to be miraculously absented from musical expression. And yet that is what the culture of classical music appreciation has attempted to do, particularly since the time of Beethoven. The gift of musical inspiration is supposed to be 'divine', coming from a higher plane. Sex and base human instinct don't exist up there; therefore great music has no truck with them. It is about 'finer things'.

But music is about our light and shade, our earthly yearnings and denials, including those below the waist. That is why we can let this purist disquiet pass us by. Frankly, the old temple could do with a bit of graffiti and a few more salacious photos. If cleavage proves as much an incentive as the name 'Schubert' in having a CD plucked off a shelf for inspection, I imagine the composer and his music are big enough to withstand the juxtaposition. Irrelevant images may be too pervasive, but they're also ephemeral. In my broadcasting experience, the intelligence of most of those new to the musical classics makes them very quick to separate the talent from the tits. Speaking of which, the aforementioned *Breasts* man, Poulenc, once wrote an essay in praise of banality. Fifty years after his death, we're adrift in a sea of it. One wonders what he would say now.

If all this searching for the sex between the notes seems too puerile or voyeuristic, rest assured it is in fact a respectable academic exercise. The eminent Sir George Grove wrote in the first edition of his *Dictionary of Music and Musicians* (1882) that 'compared with Beethoven, Schubert is as a woman to a man'. There are all sorts of implications that stem from this ambiguous comparison, and present-day musicologists haven't wasted the opportunity. The repeated wham-bam-bams at the end of Beethoven symphonies have been likened to the musical equivalent of the missionary position (have a listen to the end of the Ninth, for instance – *Ode to Joy* indeed). Schubert's more 'feminine' musical attributes remarked upon by Grove have recently been extrapolated into an imprint of gayness. Poor Schubert, outed by his crotchets. I'm not particularly interested in these arguments; wouldn't it be lovely to see them refuted by unexpected evidence: a lithograph of Beethoven in a frock, for instance?

Excess & Obsession

'Indulged in to excess, music emasculates instead of invigorating the mind.'

Plato (429–347 BC), *The Republic*

'Apart from sex I am not such a bad fellow. But I am not really interested in anything else.'

Percy Grainger, 1956

'I smoke. I drink. I stay up all night. I screw around. I'm overcommitted on all fronts.'

Leonard Bernstein, 1986

Don't think I'm quoting these as negative qualities. After all, nobody really does anything well unless they feel compelled to do it repeatedly; compulsion breeds a stronger discipline than mere obligation. Obsession is the fuel of excellence. And excess? Sometimes we need to crash through the walls of our own experience if we are ever going to know what lies beyond, since most of us are reluctant to open the door.

These are hardly new thoughts. In the 1800s the French *enfant terrible* Arthur Rimbaud was advising us that becoming a poet involved a disordering of the senses. For him, excess was a creed, and moderation a ticket to nowhere; it encouraged only staleness and mediocrity. Mind you, he gave up writing poetry before he turned twenty and took a ticket to the wilds of Africa, where he expired in his thirties. Fire in the belly is undeniably good, but beware the uncontrolled burn.

∼

Like most of the world I watched the Opening Ceremony of the Sydney 2000 Olympic Games, in which excess was the only possible vindication of a country's sporting obsession. As a classical music lover I was naturally impressed at the end when the flaming torch rose from the waters around Cathy Freeman to the strains of Berlioz's *Te Deum* (1849), one of his genuinely excessive pieces, and one we were allowed to savour for longer than planned, when the machinery stuck.

What gave me an even greater thrill was the music that accompanied the torch's final ascent to the top of the stadium: the big splashy tune at the end of Percy Grainger's 'Imaginary Ballet' *The Warriors*, completed in 1916. It was an inspired choice: a piece about 'an orgy of war-like dances, processions and merry-making' by an Australian who was an athletic, outdoorsy type, running, hiking and cartwheeling through life. The music was as virile and over-the-top as the event it crowned. Grainger would have been delighted, I suspect. He would also have felt avenged. When it was suggested that Grainger write some music for the opening of the 1956 Olympic Games in Melbourne the idea was dismissed as absurd. I was so pleased at this belated recognition of our greatest native-born musician that I rushed out to buy the CD souvenir soundtrack of the event when it was released just days later. Sadly, Grainger's music wasn't included.

There was a curious consistency in this, even forty years after his death in 1961. We still have trouble taking Percy Grainger seriously. Part of this is because he seems unimaginable as a real person; then again, such a bizarre personality could only have existed in reality. Nobody could have made him up. His excesses have such a tabloid tinge to them that he is one of the easiest composers to misrepresent. I probably do him no favours in the brief space of this book by including him in such a chapter, but it's hard to know just where else I could have put him. *Lust* perhaps (as he once wrote, 'I worship lust'), but since he considered the exercise of that lust the supreme pleasure of his life, here he is. Was he – as his 1976 biographer, John Bird, contended – 'mad'? I have no idea. But one thing is for certain: he was mummy's little boy.

RECIPE FOR AN UNUSUAL CHILDHOOD
(beginning in Melbourne, Australia, 1882)

Ingredients:
    1 syphilitic, promiscuous alcoholic father
    1 syphilitic (from husband), racially bigoted, over-protective mother with a predilection for the disciplinary horse-whip
    No siblings

Method:
- Try to blend the parents together in a typical late-Victorian marriage of convenience before having them realise some years and one child later that any combination is impossible.

- Place a statue of a Greek god at the foot of the bed during pregnancy in the hope that its remarkable qualities will magically transfer to the child.

- After birth, keep the child away from playmates his own age and instead fill his solitude with enforced piano lessons and practice.

- Add only a pinch (three months) of formal schooling.

- Avoid handling with the fingers; in fact, shun any physical contact for the first five years. After this, beat frequently with a whip.

- Allow the twelve-year-old mix to rise away from home in the warm oven of a German conservatorium.

- Promote an unnatural interdependence by keeping mother and son together at all times, ensuring that the latter continues to be beaten regularly until the age of sixteen.

- Have the mother maintain absolute control and power of veto over the son's female contacts and prospective romantic interests. Continue in this way until the son is almost forty.

Serve with lashings of... well, serve with lashings, period.

That Grainger turned out to be eccentric will hardly surprise after reading the above. Eccentric is one of the nicest adjectives we can use about him, and it marries well with the often jolly and highly idiosyncratic arrangements he made of folksongs he and others collected in Britain and Scandinavia in the first quarter of the last century. Most of us know *Country Gardens* and the *Irish Tune from County Derry* (or as it is better-known, *Danny Boy*) thanks to Grainger. Who wouldn't want to know a character with such endearing eccentricities?

» Grainger loved travelling by train, abjuring cars as much as possible after being involved in an accident. He always bought a second-class ticket and slept sitting up.

» As he grew older, he liked to sleep at home under his piano.

» He gave up eating meat in 1924 but was not fond of vegetables. A favourite food was bread and jam – no butter.

» He disliked wearing hats over his peroxided hair and often looked so unkempt that he was twice arrested for vagrancy – once as he was traversing New York's Grand Central Station carrying a metal lamp.

» He lived in the same house in White Plains, New York, for forty years but only mowed his front lawn once.

» Rather than carry a briefcase he would simply hang pens, pencils and other small items from his jacket on pieces of string.

» On some tours he preferred to hike from one engagement to another. While in South Africa in 1904 he packed a knapsack after a concert in Pietermaritzburg and walked 65 miles to his next engagement in Durban, arriving at six p.m. the following evening. On another inter-city hike, on that same tour, he was escorted by a tribe of Zulu warriors whom he encountered en route.

» During a rehearsal of Grieg's *Piano Concerto* in the Sydney Town Hall in 1934, Grainger jumped down from the platform during an orchestral passage, sprinted down the aisle to the doors at the back of the hall and made it back to the piano in time for his cadenza.

» In 1932 he told a class at New York University that the three greatest composers were Bach, Delius and Duke Ellington.

» He loved wearing shirts made of brightly coloured towelling.

» In 1928 he married his wife Ella at the end of a concert at the Hollywood Bowl before an amused audience of about 20,000. An orchestra of 126 played his work *To a Nordic Princess* (Ella was Swedish) and one of the witnesses to the ceremony was the film star Ramon Novarro. His new bride was unaware at the time that Grainger would be likely to bring out the whips during their honeymoon.

Grainger was an obsessive flagellant. He just loved his whips. The lash was his greatest sexual pleasure, and since he confessed even late in life that 'I hardly think of anything but sex', a nearby whip was an indispensable accessory. If an obliging woman was not around to take part, Grainger would happily whip himself. He documented many of his solo sessions with clinical precision, trying out various types of whip on himself and photographing the results. When he toured, his whips were packed in an extra bag for some recreation between concerts. In the early 1930s he composed an exculpatory letter to be opened in the event of he or his wife Ella dying under the lash. The sound of whipcracks meshes rather strangely with the suburban strains of *Country Gardens*.

Since the Graingers married late it was always unlikely they would have children. This is perhaps just as well, as Grainger freely admitted to having fantasies about whipping them, as well as committing incest with his daughters once they reached puberty. A resolute non-Christian, he at least made distinctions between good and evil when he declared his 'worship' of the latter. In his letters he veered constantly between self-condemnation and a defiant candour: 'I live for my lusts and I don't care if they kill me' (1930). He had felt the same way since his early teens, and even in middle age regarded himself as a 'naughty' child who 'looks to be punished for it'. It sounds like just the sort of thing his mother would have said.

∼

Rose Grainger was just a few days past her twenty-first birthday when she gave birth to Percy, and kept her youthful looks as she matured. She and her son were often mistaken for brother and sister, or even husband and wife. Certainly no marriage could have been closer; the two were inseparable throughout their sojourns in Germany,

London and the United States after leaving Melbourne in 1895. (Percy eventually took out US citizenship.)

Rose often accompanied her son on his tours as a pianist and was such a controlling presence in his romantic life that putative *amours*, realising they were always going to get two for the price of one, eventually withdrew. It was no contest; Percy considered the relationship with his mother 'the only truly passionate love affair' of his life. The intimate tone of their letters to each other could easily be mistaken for that between lovers.

So it was perhaps understandable that rumours of incest began to circulate after the end of the First World War. They were untrue, but Rose – who was already in a highly fragile state of mind after several nervous breakdowns and the effects of her encroaching syphilis – quite literally tipped over the edge. In 1922 she committed suicide by jumping out of the eighteenth-floor window of a New York office building.

~

Grainger's childhood made him more than a little twisted. It also forged one of the truly original musical minds of the twentieth century. He felt his 'Australian-ness' keenly and was empowered by it to explore the fresh air outside the hothouse of European art music of the time. He gathered up folksongs like wildflowers around Britain, Scandinavia and New Zealand and made countless arrangements of them, often with so-called 'elastic' scoring in which different combinations of instruments could be used according to circumstance. He experimented with complex rhythms and allowed players inside ensembles to wander off the common beat. He wrote for whistlers, harmoniums, ukuleles, musical glasses and big groups of 'tuneful' percussion instruments, some of which he invented. He tried to invent an electronic 'Free Music' that could ooze in any direction, just like the ripples of water fanning out from the boat that fascinated him on childhood sailing trips.

Grainger wrote that his life was 'one of kicking out into space while the world around me is dying of good taste'. This was obsession making a good point. We need the kickers and the hikers like Grainger. The whip does need to be cracked over our notions of 'good taste' that so often take us to a dead-end.

I sincerely hope that you feel emboldened to keep on sampling classical music after reading this book, but don't try to kid yourself that in so doing you have acquired 'good taste'. You should be delighted that you're sending your ears into new territory, but that's a different, and far more laudable matter. 'Good taste' is a colourless antechamber to the vast carnival of things that are possible. Good music is certainly a passport to your own special place, but that place should be one with the windows open.

Grainger never wanted the energy of his music to be confused with jollity. In fact, he said the object of his work was not to entertain, but to 'agonise'. In making his obsessions both the fuel and substance of his *oeuvre*, Percy reminds us that good music is often about bad things.

~

In 1925 Grainger listed his ideal regime for the realisation of health and talent: 'Give up all great hopes, all dislikes, all impatience, walk two to four hours daily, never smoke, never drink tea, coffee or alcohol, and always be in bed by 9.30 or 10 p.m.'

~

It's safe to say that Leonard Bernstein (1918–1990) never followed Grainger's advice. The former wonder-boy of American music – a brilliant 25-year-old conducting debutant with the New York Philharmonic in 1943, a gifted pianist, composer of everything from symphonies to musicals, and ground-breaking music educator through his television specials and concerts – Bernstein's initial excess was one of energy. In conducting circles he was at first a dashing young buccaneer among the aged and venerable; maestros were supposed to be the orchestras' tribal elders. (We're still a little suspicious of conductors without a touch of grey.) He turned the conductor into an action star, wielding his baton like a sword and launching himself into the air for the dramatic downbeats.

Bernstein was a starburst in the New York of the '40s and '50s. He was good-looking, charming and witty; the glamour-puss who whizzed up an after-show party by presiding at the piano in the company of scotch, cigarettes and other attractive young things. They loved him and he made every effort to repay them in kind. As a teenager Bernstein declared that he was going to 'try everything' in his lifetime.

Trying everything is a double-edged sword for those who seemingly have it all, especially talent. Some measure of success is guaranteed, enough to persuade that the right course has been found. And yet Bernstein was never entirely convinced: even as he excelled in one field, he began to rue his neglect of another. The paths of creator-composer versus interpreter-conductor were alternately the strongest lures. When he stepped down from the helm of the New York Philharmonic in 1969 after eleven seasons as music director he did so to concentrate on writing, but inevitably the temptation of the public's love drew him back to the podium.

The pendulum swung just as dramatically with his sexuality. Many eyebrows were raised when he married the actress Felicia Montealegre Cohn in 1951 – they had broken off their first engagement four years earlier. In 1976

Bernstein left his wife for another man, saying that 'I had to lead the rest of my life as I want'. When they reconciled a year later it was too late: Felicia was dying from cancer.

After her death in 1978 Bernstein was haunted by guilt. He felt himself responsible for his wife's illness and remembered her prediction at the time of their break-up that he would 'die a bitter and lonely old man'. Certainly during that twelve years before his own death Bernstein behaved more and more like a sybaritic pasha, often trumpeting his own excesses. In 1985 Bernstein said 'the will to love guides my living from day to day, always has, and always has messed it up to a remarkable degree, and still does'.

The 'love' that Bernstein cited was obviously a malleable concept to someone of his extraordinary intelligence. And whatever form it took, by day or night, Bernstein needed a great deal of it. The Beautiful Young Thing turned Venerated (but outrageous) Old Man could never be satisfied.

Still, in 1957 he wrote that work of genius, *West Side Story*.

~

I actually met Bernstein in 1974. He was making his one trip to Australia on a tour with the New York Philharmonic. Tickets had been snapped up the moment his concerts were announced and by the time I tried to buy a seat everything was sold out. My attempts to bribe friends or purchase a ticket from them at a hefty premium were unsuccessful. I was facing the prospect of missing Bernstein altogether.

As it turned out, the brazen confidence of a largely ignorant 17-year-old can be a powerful force. I resolved that if I couldn't see the Maestro in action I would at least let him know about this melancholy fact face-to-face.

I rang the Sydney Opera House where he was appearing, and informed the Stage Door in what would have sounded a helium-tainted voice that I was an important broadcasting executive who was despatching a courier with some important documents for Bernstein to sign. Clutching a self-typed letter of entrée I duly presented myself at the end of the concert. Somehow I persuaded both the Opera House security and Bernstein's own retinue of my veracity and was ushered into his dressing room before the inevitable horde of admirers was due to arrive.

Bernstein had just showered and was reclining in his dressing gown, a chain-smoking odalisque. Nervously, I offered him my letter, to which Bernstein, showing greater perception than his helpers, responded 'you read it'. It was a fairly pathetic 'I couldn't get in but I love your work' declaration. Bernstein listened with far more attention than it deserved. At the end of my recital he jumped up from his couch. I noticed with surprise that he was shorter than me; even in repose, he seemed almost too big for the room, and I am rather on the diminutive side.

After a brief conversation he mentioned that it was his fifty-sixth birthday and the party was beginning forthwith. The dressing room door swung open, and sparkling wine and a cake were wheeled in on a trolley followed by the official partygoers, including the then Australian prime minister, Gough Whitlam, and his wife. Bernstein introduced me to Mrs Whitlam as 'an old friend who I've just met'. I recall having a long conversation with Bernstein's nineteen-year-old son, Alexander.

The night wore on. I decided I should ring my mother to inform her of the rather obvious news that I was running late.

'Where are you?' she asked.

'I'm in Leonard Bernstein's dressing room,' I replied. 'It's his birthday.'

'Well, once he blows out the candles, you come home,' she said.

~

Here are some of your common garden excesses:

Scandal and hearsay

Nicolò Paganini (1782–1840) was a violinist of such unearthly talent and cadaverous appearance that it was said the Devil guided his bow. Paganini traded profitably on such gossip, spending the considerable proceeds on women and gambling. When his depleted system began to go downhill in 1823, a doctor presumed the cause to be syphilis and prescribed massive doses of mercury and opium cigars. The mercury poisoned his system, loosening his teeth so much that he had to tie them together with twine in order to eat. Eventually all his lower teeth were extracted (without the benefit of anaesthetic; Paganini had to be held down during the procedure) and the violinist had to support his ravaged jaw with a bandage. His public disdain for conventional morality and all the Devil talk had offended the hierarchy of the Church, who refused the deceased virtuoso's burial in consecrated ground. Instead, his corpse was embalmed, dressed in performance garb and put in a coffin with a glass pane above its face. Paganini's son was later offered 30,000 francs to exhibit the cadaver in England.

Drink

Somehow you would expect this to go with the territory. Cirrhosis was a likely contributor to Beethoven's death and the precise cause of Erik Satie's. Tchaikovsky admitted that vodka was a problem; certainly, it was a bit of a hoodoo for other Russian composers. Modest Mussorgsky (1839–1881) was a dreadful young sot who had been shaping up as one of the most original nineteenth-century composers with his opera *Boris Godunov*, the diabolic orchestral work *Night on Bare Mountain* (later to become one of the highlights of the Disney classic *Fantasia*) and the piano suite *Pictures at an Exhibition*, now a staple of the orchestral repertoire in the orchestration by Ravel. His chronic alcoholism meant that he started many more works than he finished before his premature death at the age of forty-two – a human tragedy but an even bigger tragedy for music.

The Irish-born John Field (1782–1837) was a great piano virtuoso and influential composer whose playing of his own Nocturnes captivated many a European salon and gave the young Frederic Chopin (1810–1849) more than a few ideas. Field spent a large part of his career in Russia and eventually made the bottle too much of a companion: in his forties he virtually stopped writing altogether and became known in certain circles as 'drunken John'. He asserted that the only reason he married one of his pupils was that she never paid for her lessons.

The death of Henry Purcell (1659–1695) was said to have been caused by his wife's chagrin over the number of hours he spent at the local London tavern. She locked him out of the house, causing him to spend the night in the rain and precipitating his final illness.

Women and cigarettes

These were the two favourites of Puccini's. As you'll discover in *Anger*, his amorous exploits eventually paid a grim dividend. So did the smokes; the composer was diagnosed with inoperable throat cancer in 1924 and died while receiving radiation treatment, leaving an unfinished opera, *Turandot*.

In his lifetime Puccini's celebrity and good looks led him into many a temptation. While staying in a plush Vienna hotel his fag break was interrupted by the unexpected entrance of a naked woman into his suite. Puccini thought her mad and attempted to summon the hotel staff for aid, but upon closer inspection he decided it was unwise to oppose the will of a lunatic.

Vincent Wallace (1812–1865) permitted himself (somewhat illegally) an excess of wives, contriving to be married to an Irish-woman and an American at the same time. Perhaps he was confused by the frequent travelling occasioned by a restless spirit, and a near-Wagnerian capacity for incurring debt. Wallace's itinerary included a stint in Australia during the 1830s. An outstanding pianist and violinist (he was dubbed the 'Australian Paganini'), he founded a music academy in Sydney and lived for a while at the Bush Inn in Hobart, where it is said he wrote much of what became the smash-hit opera *Maritana*, first performed in London in 1845.

A bit more flagellation

We've already touched upon the propensity to violence shown by the aristocrat/composer Gesualdo. Being a man of means, he employed ten young men to beat him three times a day. It is said that during these sessions he was 'wont to smile joyfully'.

Cat hate and facial hair

It is a relief to learn that Johannes Brahms (1833–1897) has been cleared of a century-old charge of excessive cruelty to animals. Scandalmongers put it about that Brahms would spear cats with arrows from his apartment window in Vienna, reel them up like trout, and transcribe their dying miaows into chamber music. It is now thought that these accusations of felicide were a red herring put out by Wagner, who was arguably rather too close to his dogs. And we must admire someone who was prepared to spend the last twenty years of his life dealing with the beard that Brahms thought would make a nice addition to his countenance. In fact, his face, neck and upper body ended up being almost entirely obscured. If that was the intention it is a pity, because earlier portraits and photographs show him to have been a bit of a looker. Brahms would have required some cleaning up after the soup. What a whopper. You could have lost a cat in it.

The occult, orgies and wild partying

The Englishman Philip Heseltine (1894–1930) was much attracted to black magic, as evidenced by his musical pseudonym, Peter Warlock. Completely self-taught in music, he ranged from the brooding and intensely beautiful song cycle *The Curlew* to the *Capriol Suite* for strings. He also wrote a series of *Four Codpieces* for piano. Warlock finally gassed himself at the beginning of a grim London winter.

∼

So much for the destructive excesses. These are more innocent:

SERGE PROKOFIEV (1891–1953) was once evicted from his apartment for playing the same piano chord 218 times. The downstairs tenant kept a tally.

ANTON BRUCKNER (1824–1896), the pious and unworldly Austrian organist and composer, developed a condition called numeromania that compelled him to count everything: cathedral gables, stars, leaves on trees – even the numbers of bars in his lengthy symphonies. Orchestral musicians struggling through a less than inspiring performance of Bruckner have been known to do the same; it helps to pass the time.

ERIK SATIE (1866–1925), whose static *Three Gymnopédies* for piano (1888) still sound as fresh as the day they were written, practised a defiant eccentricity that positioned him as an official laughing-stock for much of his career. His ballet *Relâche* had trouble pulling a crowd, possibly because the title translates from the French as 'this performance is cancelled'. In fact, Satie was a master of the eye-catching title appended to very short piano works: *Three Pieces in the Shape of a Pear, Desiccated Embryos, Bureaucratic Sonatina* – the list goes on. His invention of so-called 'Furniture Music' is a precursor to today's muzak, but we won't hold that against him. He lived most of his life in a drab Parisian suburb, renting the same room for nearly thirty years, into which nobody, not even the concierge, was granted entrée. He drank excessively, a legacy of his earlier cabaret-hopping life in Montmartre, but lived frugally, save for a couple of obsessive indulgences: seven identical velvet suits, constituting his entire wardrobe, plus a collection of umbrellas.

GIACOMO ROSSINI (1792–1868) could either go like a chainsaw or barely leave his bed. Sometimes he could do both at the same time. One story had him churning out the pages on a lazy day between the sheets. A page slipped to the floor, and rather than leave his cocoon to pick it up, Rossini simply wrote out a new one.

The sheer speed and facility this suggests was no musical urban myth. He wrote his comic opera *The Barber of Seville* (1816) in less than a fortnight (albeit with a bit of recycling here and there) and suggested that the best incentive to work was to 'wait until the evening before opening night'. Even this deadline was too loose for Rossini at times. The Overture to his opera *The Thieving Magpie* (1817) was written on the very day of the work's premiere, with Rossini locked in a room at the theatre by stagehands who collected the sheets of newly inscribed manuscript as they came sailing out from a window.

These brief periods of slavery paid off handsomely for Rossini. He was world-famous in his early twenties and collected the cash to match. Of all the composers in this book he was probably the wealthiest, building homes in several European cities and hosting celebrated salons in later life. Paying for his next meal was not a problem when he elected to retire at the age of thirty-seven, which was just as well, because he loved his food and even lent his creativity to cuisine, inventing the dish 'Tournedos Rossini'.

To have written the sparkling, witty music the world still loves (a recording of Rossini overtures will always add champagne to your collection), to have been a famous dispenser of *bon mots*, to have become the most famous name in European music, and then opt for an early and opulent retirement, would suggest a contented life. Not so, for Rossini was prey to such severe depression that writers today have suggested he suffered from a bipolar disorder. Mood swings, money, talent, celebrity; all put to marvellous purpose, but almost too much for a single life.

The second half of Rossini's life (his 'retirement') lasted longer than the first and he soldiered on as a living legend into his late seventies.

Big Opera

Motorists who gasp in wonder at Australian roadside apparitions like the Big Banana were born 350 years too late to savour the gigantism of Antonio Cesti's (1623–1669) opera *The Golden Apple*. Cesti veered from the sacred to the secular in his lifestyle, being both a Franciscan monk and an operatic tenor in his native Italy, before his burgeoning stage career and habit of dropping the habit when in the company of sopranos forced an exit from the monastery after his superiors excoriated his 'dishonourable and irregular life'. We don't know what he looked like, but his personality was obviously one that irritated his competitors in the music world, to the point that his early death was attributed to poison. Being a composer was dangerous in the seventeenth century.

One hopes Cesti didn't succumb to bad fruit. It would have been an irony given the success of his huge *Apple*, staged at the Viennese royal court in 1668. It was by far the most costly opera of its time, requiring twenty-four complete sets depicting everything from the underworld to the home of the gods. In between there were forests, flying dragons, storms at sea and people descending from clouds, all in a new theatre purpose-built for the performances in a Baroque cross between Wagner's Bayreuth and Las Vegas. Cesti had warmed up for this epic by composing an equestrian ballet the year before.

But when one talks about 'big opera' the popular favourite is Verdi's *Aida*, first performed at the Cairo Opera House in 1871 and obligingly set in ancient Egypt. The exotic locale gives the cue for ambitious producers to dig deep for the décor, particularly in the open-air productions that seem to suit this opera so well. You can have it all: virtual pyramids, a Sphinx or two, a chorus of Egyptians stretching to the horizon and the cavalcade of horses and elephants whose onstage critiques of the show have littered much theatrical legend and left many skid-marks. It's said that Noël Coward sat through a performance that featured both an incontinent elephant and a less than satisfactory soprano in the lead; he later remarked that the night's problems would have been solved by shoving the singer's head up the animal's backside.

The French called the genre *grand opéra* and it certainly spent much of the nineteenth century on this elephantine scale. King of the heap, the nineteenth-century version of Andrew Lloyd Webber, was Giacomo Meyerbeer (1791–1864) whose colossal operas became tourist attractions. Audiences loved the action in the crowd scenes (the more violent the better) and the special effects. We haven't changed, really. Meyerbeer operas always have hordes of soldiers, peasants and monks. The soldiers try to kill the peasants and the monks try to mediate, resulting in their own deaths. Much blood is spilt over timpani rolls and roaring brass, not a drop touching the orchestra. The Huguenots in his 1836 opera of that name are massacred by the Protestants in sixteenth-century Paris, sinful nuns are raised from the dead for a Bacchanal in *Robert the Devil* (1831), and Vasco da Gama's entire crew is massacred aboard ship during a storm at sea in *The African Woman* (1865). Even too much is never enough: the entire cast is wiped out in an explosion at the end of *The Prophet* (1849). With an outcome like that, I'd be looking for a better prophet.

Of course, with Richard Wagner and his *Ring* cycle these explosions are mere penny crackers in the firework display of existence. He wrote about nothing less than all-out apocalypse (see *Triumph*).

Excessive Notes

There have been few if any composers as prolific as Georg Philipp Telemann (1681–1767). He wrote thousands of works for every instrument, in every genre, and in every known European national style, achieving all this from a standing start, given that he was almost completely self-taught.

Telemann's first wife, a lady-in-waiting, died in childbirth fifteen months after their wedding. His second wife, the daughter of a Frankfurt council clerk, was made of sterner stuff; she produced eight sons and two daughters. It would seem that she was more than a match for her husband's prodigious energy. While he took time out from reproductive duties to pen another one of his 1,400 cantatas or 125 or so concertos (to name a few), Mrs Telemann took up with a Swedish officer and eventually fled Hamburg in the company of her new man, leaving her husband with massive gambling debts. The scandal was the talk of the town and became the subject of a satirical play that was banned by the authorities. Poor cuckolded Telemann applied a grim humour to his situation, appealing for financial aid from friends with a letter that began 'My lot is now much easier to bear. Extravagance departed with my spouse'.

The most famous story on this matter concerns Mozart. We know this to be true because it was even included in the film *Amadeus*. After a rehearsal of his new opera *The Abduction from the Seraglio* in 1781, the Austrian Emperor Joseph II bailed up the composer with the comment that there were 'too many notes'. The confident 25-year-old replied that there were exactly as many notes as required.

Excess is in the ear of the listener.

A Final Word

In the end, who can really judge how much is too much? One can also become obsessed with these flaws and distortions in composers' personalities and I see that this part of the book has run to excessive length. Are such life details irrelevant to the main game of the music itself?

For me, they simply underline the miracle of the music's existence. Music has to bump and grind its way to the cruel air of the outside world. People create because, in the end, they just can't help themselves, but being contrary creatures of remarkable imagination, their personal peccadilloes can sometimes prove the biggest obstacles of all. The great ones will always push through; think of all the perfectly good music we will never hear because the person with the idea thought they would start work tomorrow. Perhaps in another dimension there is a place full of postponed sonatas.

Mozart may have loved his all-night parties and billiards, and he blew a few career opportunities by rubbing people up the wrong way, but you couldn't call him a slacker. The real fruit of our composers' penchant for excess and obsession is what they have left to us, and what they continue to write. Even if this chapter has documented some of the collateral damage, we are still getting the better end of the deal.

∼

In the delicate matter of love, obsession nurtures expectations. In imagining they have been fulfilled, we feel the rush of conquest, of all-out triumph, and press on further into the affair.

Triumph

'The whole will become the greatest work of poetry ever written.'

Richard Wagner about his *Ring* cycle

It is one of life's greatest, and most petty satisfactions: to be proved right.

In Charlie Chaplin's autobiography there is a story of an early dramatic encounter with classical music. In 1913, while still an unknown stage comedian touring the United States with an English vaudeville troupe, the 24-year-old took a few days off from the grind of provincial shows to make a solo trip to New York. This oasis of comparative luxury included a good hotel, half a bottle of champagne and a first time visit to the opera, Wagner's *Tannhäuser* (1845) at the Metropolitan. Chaplin knew neither German nor anything about the opera's plot, yet when the Pilgrim's Chorus began in Act Three, the future Little Tramp found himself weeping uncontrollably. 'What people sitting next to me must have thought I don't know,' he wrote. 'The music seemed to sum up all the travail of my life.' World celebrity for Chaplin as a film comedian was only a few months away.

Whether or not Chaplin sensed a kindred spirit, he was to return to Wagner much later in his film *The Great Dictator*, a daring spoof on Hitler released at the beginning of the Second World War. Perhaps he knew of Hitler's Wagnerian passion. For a comedy, it is a uniquely chilling moment: when the dictator dreams of universal domination he performs a balloon dance with a globe of the world to the ethereal strains of Wagner's Act I Prelude to *Lohengrin*. What an unlikely trio of control freaks – the actor, the demented autocrat and the composer. Each in his own way wished to manufacture a complete and detailed world, running to its own rules, while insisting we all come along for the ride. Chaplin's was the world of the past. Wagner and Hitler saw themselves as emissaries of the future.

∼

There are two good reasons for not including Richard Wagner in this book. The most obvious is that he hardly needs the exposure; more words have been written about

Wagner than about any other figure in musical history. He also leads the field as the recipient of spleen, hyperbole, imitation and analysis.

The second is that this modest tome is an attempt to relate states of mind and emotion experienced by some of history's great composers to those we experience today, so that we can compare our responses with theirs and follow, or avoid, their example. Composers are like us, in other words.

This is an implausible claim in the case of Wagner. He was definitely not normal, and of all the composers he is the one who can make the listener feel most insignificant. There is virtually nothing in his life, behaviour or achievement that suggests the everyday. His charm could completely seduce women from the arms of their husbands. His temper was frightening and easily inflamed. His grief over the death of the household dog was debilitating (possibly his most human trait). And his self-belief enabled him to triumph against every setback in the book: poverty, indifference, hostility, exile and subterfuge. Long after any mortal would have given up, Wagner kept faith in himself and his work, sustained by the credo that he was the greatest musician in the world. His father-in-law (and biggest fan) Franz Liszt said 'in the matter of glory Wagner fasted for thirty years'. In his sixties, that fast broke; Wagner was proved right. He had triumphed.

When our confidence in ourselves suffers a series of painful low blows it takes a sturdy constitution not to be deflected from long-term goals. Wagner's absence of doubt would almost be classified as that of a megalomaniac, were it not for the fact that he actually fulfilled his intentions and persevered for as long as it took. His *Ring* cycle occupied twenty-eight years (1848–1876), from conception to first complete performance in a new theatre built according to the composer's specifications, during which time Wagner had revolutionised Western music with his *Tristan and Isolde*. His quote at the head of this chapter, outlandish as it must have seemed at the time, was prophetic; the *Ring* is certainly one of the most influential works of poetry ever written. But what sort of person could make such a claim on his own behalf in the first place?

Not a particularly pleasant one. Being merely 'pleasant' was never his intention. That was part of the make-up of Mr Average. 'I am not made like other people,' he insisted, 'the world owes me what I need'. In the end the world gave it to him, but only after a lifetime of asking. Nobody ever demanded charity with such self-assurance. Imagine a letter arriving out of the blue from a comparative stranger saying something like 'Give us a few quid, could you? I'm knocking out the greatest poem ever written. Do you have a spare bed for a couple of months? You'll find my company irresistible. Congratulations – I don't offer these privileges to just anyone.' In a nutshell, this was a typical Wagner spiel. You'd be careful about saying yes, I suspect. Some did and lived to regret it.

∼

Wagner was born in Leipzig, Germany, in 1813. His father died six months later. His mother had been friendly with a local actor and married him only nine months after being widowed. Many have suggested that the actor, Ludwig Geyer, was Wagner's biological father after all.

When your teenager suddenly declares a life ambition that bears no relation to his sphere of knowledge, don't laugh. Little Richard (he was short) decided to become a composer at the age of fifteen after hearing Beethoven's Ninth Symphony, experiencing a revelatory thunderbolt and thereafter behaving as if fired from a gun. But Wagner was a non-performer at school and completely untrained in music; he may as well have said that he was going to walk to the moon. Even with such dedicated zeal his musical studies were sketchy at best. He could only pick at the piano, played no other instrument, and was a so-so score reader. Somehow, it didn't matter. Wagner took what he needed and allowed gut instinct to refine the rest. Still fifteen, he wrote a play modelled after Shakespeare called

Leubald, which killed off so many of the large cast they had to be brought back as ghosts in order to speak the final lines. Maturity never taught him greater restraint.

Wagner drank and gambled his way through an incomplete university course, and wrote a symphony that had audiences in hysterics. He secured a job as a musical director in a small German town called Magdeburg in 1834, beginning a pattern of incurring enormous debts and then leaving town when the creditors came calling. Wagner spent money all his life like there was no tomorrow. He wrote 'I can't live on a miserable pittance!', to which others would have responded 'Who does he think he is, a genius?' Well – *yes.*

He fell in love with an actress called Minna Planer and married her in 1836. She was already a mother, having been seduced at fifteen by an army captain. Six months after marrying Wagner she decamped with a businessman. The newlyweds were eventually reunited, but Minna had to endure Wagner's subsequent jealousy even as he pursued his own affairs. After one escape from one bankruptcy too many the pair snuck off to Paris in 1839 and lived like paupers for the next two-and-a-half years. Wagner was reduced to making piano arrangements of musical trash to put bread on the table; he even suffered a spell in a debtor's prison.

Wagner was down, but he didn't crack. In Paris he completed *The Flying Dutchman,* a seafaring ghost story about redemption through love – a favourite theme of Wagner's. The Overture from the opera presents an astonishing example of the sense of power developing in his music, as it evokes a storm at sea, the wind howling in the rigging, the crash of the waves against the hull. This is no mere picture painting; there is an elemental quality about it. This is no representation of nature. It *is* a force of nature (fellow composer Charles Gounod called it a 'hurricane'), charged with a take-no-prisoners attitude that rampages through his subsequent work.

For sheer sonic impact Wagner is like going to a rock concert. 'Listening' is too passive a response; instead, one has to submit. Charm has nothing to do with it. An audience just has to decide whether or not it wants to be slapped around until it likes the sensation. Many did not. The printed vitriol that was poured upon Wagner's work from the 1840s would fill several entertaining volumes by itself. It also makes you wonder how anybody these days would survive such constant bucketing.

Wagner: The Critics Raved!

'Inspired by the riots of cats scampering around an ironmonger's shop in the dark.'

Alexandre Dumas père

'An old Italian painting of a martyr whose intestines are slowly unwound from his body on a reel.'

Eduard Hanslick

'A sort of chromatic moan.'

Hector Berlioz

'An endlessly ruminating monster afflicted with a revolting eructation.'

Ludwig Speidel

'Affected, sapless, soulless, beginningless, endless, topless, bottomless, topsy-turviest, tongs-and-boniest doggerel.'

John Ruskin

'Wagner's art is diseased.'

Friedrich Nietzsche

There is so much more.

Beware The Smart Man Who Asks For Money

Fortunately, Wagner had his supporters, and they sometimes responded in spectacular fashion to his frequent calls for assistance. The dénouments from some of these situations show the dangers inherent in extending charity to genius. Three examples demonstrate Wagner's repayment to a helping hand:

» *Franz Liszt, the mid-nineteenth-century Power Man of music, championed Wagner in print and performance, conducting the premiere of Lohengrin in 1850.*

Wagner, only two years Liszt's junior, responded by becoming his son-in-law after fathering three children by Liszt's daughter, Cosima, while she was inconveniently married to someone else.

» *Otto Wesendonck, wealthy silk merchant, lent Wagner money during the 1850s and allowed him to live on one of his Swiss estates at a vastly reduced rent.*

Wagner conducted a passionate affair (possibly not consummated) with Wesendonck's wife Mathilde. The interception of their love letters by Wagner's wife in 1858 precipitated the final rupture in the composer's own marriage. (She had endured numerous other affairs of Wagner's; in 1850, he almost eloped to the Orient with another young admirer.) The musical fallout of the Wesendonck episode resulted in perhaps the most influential opera ever composed, *Tristan and Isolde* about, of all things, a passionate affair. When Mr Wesendonck tactfully purchased some of Wagner's manuscripts, enabling the composer to move on, Wagner went to Paris and set himself up in high style, employing a servant and a valet, and paying the rent three years in advance.

» *In 1864 the teenage, gay and incipiently mad King Ludwig II of Bavaria responded to Wagner's printed appeal for financial aid by giving him carte blanche to produce his works in Munich and an almost unlimited supply of funds for living expenses. The first big event to come from this was the premiere of* Tristan and Isolde *in 1865, conducted by Hans von Bülow.*

Wagner went overboard with extravagance. His spell over the adoring King aroused the opposition of the court and he was pressured into leaving Munich in 1865. Still clutching the King's gift of an open chequebook, Wagner installed himself at a palatial estate on Lake Lucerne, spending everyone else's money (in Wagnerese, his due worth) on necessary opulence: silks, furs, perfumes, wallpaper of yellow leather traced in gold or violet velvet, orientalia and immaculate gardens. As he said, 'I must have brilliance and beauty and light.' In return for Maestro Bülow's worshipful service on the podium, Wagner took

Mrs Bülow as his mistress. Ludwig eventually went completely insane and drowned himself in 1886.

What is remarkable about all the exploited donors listed above is the extent of their magnanimity. Bülow, while the subject of international humiliation over his cuckolding, almost congratulated his estranged wife on her involvement with a 'higher order of being'. Wagner's acolytes believed – one might say *still* believe – in him with the sort of fervour we associate these days with religious cults. And in a sense, this *was* a religion: the new religion of Art. All that remained was to build a home temple, a shrine to Wagner's art and the natural dwelling place of Wagner's immense cycle *The Ring of the Nibelung* completed in 1874: a fifteen-hour epic in instalments that takes four nights to perform. And incredibly, this was achieved in the German town of Bayreuth by 1876, thanks to help from subscriptions, Wagner's concert fees and a generous handout from the white-knight King. The so-called Festival Theatre is the architectural incarnation of Wagner's ideas about 'music-drama' (no longer the prosaic form called 'opera') and theatre design. It is still one of the acoustic marvels of the world, with a hooded pit masking the huge orchestra from the audience's sightline while deflecting the sound onto the vast stage, where the singers can cast their voices on top like flowers on the sea. Even in the twenty-first century, going to the Bayreuth Festival remains the supreme music theatre experience for thousands of artistic pilgrims.

Want To Stick Around?

Start a dynasty, live long and breed late – this appears to be the reproductive credo of the Wagner clan. Consider this: Wagner was born in 1813. Named after the hero of the *Ring* cycle then being written, his only son Siegfried was born in 1869 when Richard was fifty-six. Wagner Senior died in early 1883 in his seventieth year and Siegfried was inexorably drawn into the family musical tradition after studies in architecture and travels through India and China. I do feel more than a tinge of sympathy for Siegfried Wagner, named after an operatic hero and the only son of such an extraordinary father; it might have been safer to stay in the Orient designing pagodas.

Richard's widow Cosima survived him by nearly fifty years; she died in 1930. Siegfried married only in 1915 to an Englishwoman, Winifred, who was nearly thirty years his junior. A formidable personality, more Wagnerian than her husband, she pursued a friendship with Hitler, who was one of the biggest Wagner groupies. Winifred survived her husband by another fifty years, right through to 1980, nearly one hundred years after the death of her father-in-law.

Siegfried and Winifred's two sons, Wieland and Wolfgang, both made their careers in the family 'business' by taking over the Bayreuth Festival after the Second World War and mounting innovative productions of their grandfather's works. Wieland died in 1966, but Wolfgang clung tenaciously to the artistic reins of the Wagner shrine until shortly before his death in 2010, when control was handed to his two daughters in an uneasy family truce. The older of the two, Eva Wagner-Pasquier, stepped down in mid-2015, leaving the Festival solely in the hands of the composer's great-grand-daughter Katharina, who was born as recently as 1978 (Wolfgang keeping the late-fatherhood tradition alive). For decades the Wagner clan has been splintering and fighting over the line of succession; the history of Richard's rabid anti-Semitism and his daughter-in-law Winifred's friendship with Hitler hanging over them like a ghastly mantle, much like the squabbling of gods, giants and gnomes over power and gold in the *Ring* cycle. And Wagner tells us what happened to them.

～

Music's other triumphant career belongs to Wagner's contemporary, the Italian Giuseppe Verdi (1813–1901). More than one hundred years after his death he is still the most-performed opera composer in the world, and the company that is brave enough *not* to include some Verdi in its annual season will have a hard time at the box-office. His is the ultimate operatic list of hits, including *Rigoletto* (1851), *La traviata* (1853), *Il trovatore* (1853), *Aida* (1871) and *Otello* (1887).

Verdi's talent was not initially apparent to those who should have known better. When the teenager Verdi came in from the provinces to audition for the prestigious Milan Conservatory in 1832, he was rejected. According to the authorities, Giuseppe was a foreigner, too old, and played the piano with his hands in an incorrect position. The composer never learned of these reasons in his lifetime. Years later, this same institution asked Verdi for permission to be named after him. He was not amused by the gall of a club wanting to adopt the title of someone they had not wanted as a member (to misquote Groucho Marx). 'They didn't want me young. They cannot have me old,' he said.

By the late 1830s the young composer was happily married with two young children, a girl and a boy. Having secured a good private musical education after his Conservatory rejection, he was struggling to make his way with the promise of an opera to be staged at Milan's La Scala. Then, catastrophe: within the space of two years Verdi lost his entire family to illness. When his wife completed this sad trio of deaths in June 1840, the composer was in the throes of writing, of all things, a comedy called *Un giorno di regno* ('King for a Day'). Under these circumstances one can only begin to imagine Verdi's enthusiasm for humour, so it is understandable that the premiere was a disaster and the opera was withdrawn as soon as the curtain came down to shouts of derision.

The shattered composer vowed never to write music again and became a virtual recluse, taking his meals occasionally at a nearby trattoria. One winter evening, the snow falling thickly, Verdi bumped into the Director of La Scala in the street during a solitary walk. Signor Merelli dragged the reluctant composer aside and forced on him a libretto for his consideration. On returning to his lodgings, Verdi says he threw the manuscript onto the table 'with a violent gesture'. It fell open at the line '*Va pensiero, sull'ali dorate*' ('Fly, thought, on golden wings') sung by the captive Hebrew slaves in ancient Babylon under the reign of Nebuchadnezzar.

That was it; inspiration burst into life, and Verdi became instantly famous when his completed opera *Nabuco* opened in 1842 with the Chorus of the Hebrew Slaves as the showstopper. He never looked back, and died a national hero nearly sixty years later. '*Va pensiero*' is still his most famous melody.

The Frenchman Georges Bizet (1838–1875) once said that 'Wagner is Verdi with the addition of style'. The best invective heaped upon composers has come from their peers. Bizet himself was killed by indifference, some say, when his masterpiece *Carmen* opened to a glacial reception and an overwhelmingly hostile press in March 1875. He had taken the genre of *opéra-comique*, which interspersed singing with dialogue and was considered a vehicle for humorous and satirical subjects, and turned it over to a story of seduction and sexual jealousy set in sunny Spain; Carmen herself is stabbed to death by her spurned and demented lover during a bullfight. The audience, not receiving their expected jolly night out, sat on their hands. Bizet paced the street outside the theatre saying 'this time I am really sunk.'

Depression paved the way for illness and the composer passed away the following June as Carmen continued to play to half-empty houses. He was thirty-six. Four months later a triumphant production in Vienna started the opera on its way around the world. Today it is up there with Puccini's *La bohème* as the genre's number one hit. *Carmen* was Tchaikovsky's favourite opera, and the philosopher (and former Wagner acolyte) Nietzsche hailed the work as a sort of clarifying Wagnerian antidote.

All too late for its composer.

By the time of the 1905 Prix de Rome, 29-year-old Maurice Ravel was considered by many to be one of France's most talented composers, excepting the eminent judges of the Paris Conservatoire, where Ravel studied on and off for fourteen years. The competition for composers was considered highly prestigious and the first prize included a stint of completely subsidised residence in the Eternal City; previous winners had included Berlioz, Bizet and Debussy. Ravel had flunked out in his previous three attempts and this entry would be his last, as he had hit the age limit. Rumour had it that his ascension was a formality.

Instead, Ravel was knocked out in the preliminary round. *Scandale!* Parisian musical society was outraged and the controversy could only be quelled by the resignation of the Conservatoire's director. Ravel went sailing with friends in Holland. Somebody somewhere might know the names of the Conservatoire judges in 1905, but most people know who wrote the *Bolero*.

The Brat Johann

Finally, the traditional family battleground of father versus son, or the Strauss Affair.

Take two Johanns in old Vienna: father (born 1804) and son (born 1825). Father made a success by fanning the new dance craze, the waltz, and playing his own compositions with his own orchestra. Johann Senior also sired a total of thirteen children; six of these with his wife, and a second, larger family of love children with his mistress. It was common enough for an unmusical father to disapprove of a son's artistic leanings for fear that the life of a musician was impecunious, even disreputable, but the elder Johann, although a successful musician, felt much the same way and tried to steer his first-born into a career as a banker.

The Strauss genes would not be so easily suppressed and young Johann dropped his bookkeeping studies in 1842 in favour of music. His father immediately detected the prospect of a competitor in the family ('the brat Johann also intends to write waltzes although he has not got a clue about them'), but was powerless to halt the surge of public interest in the emergence of another Kapellmeister Strauss. The young Johann's début at Dommayer's Casino in October 1844 was an immediate success.

Johann I died in 1849, having made a big musical career from humble origins in the suburbs of Vienna. The son he tried to keep away from a professional music life became the Strauss who dominated European light music in the second half of the nineteenth century, wrote the immortal *Blue Danube* waltz (1867) and was eventually dubbed 'The Waltz King'.

TRIUMPH

Ah, the spoils of victory. When all has capitulated in your favour in music or love there comes a chapter where one can settle back to savour the heady wine.

Joy

'Great art can be happy as well as tragic. The time for any serious effort is past.'

Emmanuel Chabrier

Music should exist only when it is absolutely necessary not to have silence. When you've heard as much music as I have, the restless mind becomes an endless storehouse of recollected sound that fires up on long walks in remote places. When one should be opening the ears up to nature's symphony of wind, bird song, distant running water, instead – prompted by the rhythm of tramping feet – I hear a medley of Western art music's Top 300. Slow movements don't match my mood; I pour my exhilaration into a spontaneous mental soundtrack that acquires more trombones, crashing cymbals and speed with each successive hilltop.

I took a sabbatical in 1999 to live for a couple of months in a small town in southern France. After a while I managed to look as indolent as the rest of its seemingly unemployed populace. Long days were wasted in the contemplation of a paragraph over a *demi-litre* of anything intoxicating. On days when I wanted to feel 'productive', opening up the windows of a former self to release the stale odours of a Protestant work ethic, I would take a track that wound precipitously behind the village into what was called the Sea of Rock. Within a twist or two of its serpentine track all trace of living civilisation was erased, giving way to silence, limestone outcrops and long-abandoned stone farmhouses battered to ruins by encroaching scrub.

One particular morning I decided to keep going on to the next town, a good ten kilometres away along the top of a nearby escarpment, necessitating a long climb. The day was glorious, and the composers kept me wonderful company as I ascended. At the highest point of the walk, standing close to a cliff edge, fanned by the wind and looking at the distant Cévennes mountains, I felt actively happy, exultant. And whose music surged through my cerebellum to fit the moment? Monsieur Emmanuel Chabrier.

∼

The association of Chabrier's music with high altitudes is very appropriate. He was a mountain man, born in the

Auvergne region of France in 1841. Perhaps as a child he heard some of the folksongs of the area that would become so famous in Joseph Canteloube's orchestral arrangements nearly a hundred years later.

Chabrier was a musically gifted child, but as the son of a lawyer these proclivities were considered frivolous. Therefore, he studied law, graduating in 1861 and taking a job in the French Ministry of the Interior, where he remained a government employee for nearly twenty years.

There are valuable lessons for us in Chabrier's life and art:

Life's profundity is measured in laughs as much as tears

'Stop laughing, this is serious!' is a phrase I remember from orchestral rehearsals back in my days as a music student. We have been persuaded that the deep and meaningful belongs to drama and a furrowed brow.

When Chabrier moved to Paris from the provinces in 1856, the City of Light was the home of grand opera at its grandest; personal tragedies in historic settings with big sets, big choruses, impossible love, betrayal and death. This was the meat of art; comedies were the dessert, and therefore, of less consequence.

Chabrier found this intolerable. 'Art with a capital

letter, serious Art, is bogged down and stagnating,' he wrote to a friend. Why was a frown more important? He was drawn to comedy. In his early twenties, fresh out of law school, he began writing two operettas with his friend, the poet Paul Verlaine. In the 1870s he completed two 'light' stage works: *L'étoile* (1877, something of a masterpiece) and *Une éducation manquée* ('An Incomplete Education').

Much later, one of his few orchestral works, the *Joyous March* (1888), had the orchestra in stitches during its first rehearsal. This wasn't laughter of derision; the players had simply tuned in to the music's exuberance. Chabrier's most-performed piece is his orchestral rhapsody *España* (1883), a souvenir of a holiday with his family on the Iberian peninsula during which the composer confessed in ribald fashion to a fascination with women's swimwear. One can imagine his eyeballs popping out on those Spanish beaches. *España* explodes from the orchestra in good performance. The composer Vincent d'Indy called him 'the angel of drollery', but there are no mere giggles in Chabrier's earthy score; the laughter comes from deep in the solar plexus.

Chabrier tells us that while life's vicissitudes can be laughed at or wept over, one of these options is by far the healthier. What Leonard Bernstein called 'the joy of music' was Chabrier's point of entry. For the self-declared 'clog-dancing Auvergnat' (a reference to his unpretentious country origins) music was the earth under our feet, the curve of a woman waist-deep in water, the colours of a painting by one of his Impressionist friends, attacking the ivories with gusto – he was famed as 'a slayer of pianos' – and a good rollicking dance; the spice in what turned out for him to be a short life. Syphilis took him at only fifty-three; during his decline the formerly boisterous composer eventually conceded that not even his Muse could save him. He wrote 'poor dear music, my poor dear friend, so you no longer want me to be happy? I love you though, and I rather think you'll be the death of me.'

Trust your midlife crisis, it's telling you something

In 1880 Chabrier was thirty-nine, a respectable public servant in the Ministry of the Interior, happily married with two sons, a perfect picture of nine-to-five bourgeois respectability. True, he consorted with artsy friends, knocked out loud piano music at parties and dabbled with comic operas, but since he'd never attended a music conservatory these were considered merely amateur pursuits.

In that same year Chabrier was taken to Munich by friends to hear Wagner's *Tristan and Isolde*. The experience proved cathartic. Chabrier was sobbing just minutes into the Prelude. Some hurried examination of his life's purpose must have followed. The results were dramatic; two months short of his fortieth birthday he gave up a completely secure job, let what was left of his hair down and took the plunge into the financially uncertain puddle of freelance composition.

His immediate circle was concerned for him because his children were still young, and the middle-aged lawyer possessed no formal musical qualifications. Heaven knows what was going on in his head; perhaps a presentiment or even a first symptom of his long, degenerative illness prompting the thought that time was passing. Almost certainly there was the same struggle between yearning and social-familial responsibility that we all experience. These days when one is thirty-nine or thereabouts such an impulsive roll of the dice is tagged a 'mid-life crisis'.

Since this was 1880 and not a hundred years later, Chabrier could not seek the advice of psychiatrists, financial advisors, lifestyle columnists, radio chat shows or self-help books – much less this one. All would doubtless have told him that his plan was a folly attributable to 'that' time of life. Think of the damage he would have done to his superannuation! In his own time there would have been plenty of anxious muttering from in-laws, friends, the gang at the Home Office.

As it turns out, Chabrier was right to take the punt. His time was short. There would be little more than ten years left to him to follow his passion. And if the doubting Thomases had prevailed, the world would have had one less great composer to tell us something valuable about joy. Chabrier's dilemma, even the decision he took, is common these days; the consequences of that decision decidedly not. They are the glorious musical dividends of a risk-taker. We should all be so lucky to have such a crisis.

*The right path for you is usually
the most obvious*

Falling under Wagner's spell was a catalyst that liberated Chabrier. Falling *victim* to the spell was dangerously close to another form of servitude. Chabrier's infatuation morphed into attempts to emulate, if not downright imitate, the German master. In spite of his proclivity for wit and fast-paced stage comedy, for intimacy and the short punchy musical message, he decided to write large dramatic operas with quasi-mythic settings à la *Tristan*: *Gwendoline* (1886), starring the Saxons and the Danes in ninth-century Britain, and the unfinished *Briséïs*, a Christian versus Pagan version of *Sophie's Choice*, set even further back, in the first century AD, which could now perhaps be completed by Ridley Scott.

Having jumped in the right car, much time was wasted in driving down the wrong road. Perhaps this was his notion of what a 'serious' composer did. There isn't much modern regard for these long-winded excursions against the grain. What an irony for Chabrier after all his early railing against 'Serious' Art!

The old one about the company we keep

Chabrier would be at my Ultimate Dinner Party. He may not have had Oscar Wilde's class of wit or Wagner's charisma, but there must have been something about this short, balding, paunchy character that endeared him to many in the artistic milieu of Paris. He fell in with a group of literary types called *Le Parnasse,* who maintained a sort of HQ in a café.

An early friend and artistic collaborator was the great poet Paul Verlaine, who later wrote a sonnet about Chabrier. Painters were conspicuous in his circle and he paid them the supreme compliment of purchasing their works, including Monet, Renoir, and Cézanne. Manet's famous *A Bar at the Folies Bergère* used to hang above Chabrier's piano; the painter later died in his arms. He also enjoyed the friendship of other composers, such as Fauré, Chausson, Saint-Saëns and Massenet – the ones at the time who counted. His close friend Duparc dragged him on that fateful pilgrimage to Munich to hear *Tristan*. On a later visit to Bayreuth he was invited to tea by Wagner's widow Cosima and brought little distinction upon himself by quietly discarding his cake into a chest of drawers.

By all accounts, collecting this glittering assembly of France's greatest artistic figures wasn't status-driven; these were genuine friendships built on mutual esteem. His music is just as endearing and evokes the composer's personality to those who came after. In the 1920s the French composer Francis Poulenc put a coin into an early version of the jukebox in Paris. Out came a piano piece called *Idylle* by Chabrier, whom Poulenc had believed to be a minor composer. He later wrote 'even today it makes me tremble with emotion to think of the resultant miracle. My music has never forgotten that first kiss. Dear Chabrier, how we all love you!'

~

Odes to Joy

Joy's most famous anthem would have to be that of Beethoven's setting of Schiller's *Ode to Joy* in the final movement of his Ninth Symphony (1824). It was a spectacular innovation at the time, the expression of a feeling so great that the instruments-only model of a symphony cracked like a redundant Berlin Wall to allow voices to come rushing through. They sang it in Germany to celebrate that very event in 1989, and in Japan there are hundreds of annual performances of the work. Joy is confined in the famous tune to a span of essentially five notes, and yet it seems to open out to enfold the world.

Another world resounding with joy is evoked in the orchestral suite *The Planets,* by the English-born Gustav Holst (1874–1934). Leaving the earth out of the musical picture, this serenade to outer space has been used frequently for dramatic signatures in TV shows about war and, well, outer space. *Jupiter, the Bringer of Jollity* is a galumphing piece whose percolating textures settle down at one point for one of those 'big' tunes that soon turned into the anthem *I Vow to Thee, My Country*. This became a staple at football matches, weddings (Princess Diana's) and, a little strangely, funerals (Churchill's and, yes, Princess Diana's).

While nothing unites a crowd better than a song, many notes have been spent in the expression of life's smaller pleasures. Johann Sebastian Bach composed hundreds of sacred cantatas; my own favourite is a secular one in which a rebellious daughter brags of her fondness, yea verily, her *addiction* for coffee in the so-called *Coffee Cantata* (1734). What one hopes to be a more private pleasure is vented by the Swiss-born Ludwig Senfl (c1486–1543) in a song about breaking wind in the bath.

Drinking is a popular musical topic. Goblets are raised in the tavern scene of many an opera. If the characters are too highborn to nick off to the pub they drink at home with a multitude of friends. In Italian opera a drinking song is a Brindisi, of which the most famous example is that in Verdi's *La traviata*. England's King Henry VIII (1491–1547) was undoubtedly a popular man, having almost as many friends as he did wives, and he celebrated the good times in a great song called *Pastyme with good companye*.

George Gershwin's (1898–1937) little *Promenade* also rejoices under the title *Walking the Dog*. Other ankle-biters feature in operas and instrumental 'nursery' suites, one of the most beautiful being Bizet's *Children's Games* of 1871. The small hero of Rossini's *Song of the Baby* does what babies do so many times a day and reports the *caca* to Daddy with that very word. Perhaps Rossini took some pleasure in infantilism, given that the song features in his late collection *Sins of Old Age*.

In Praise Of Gratitude

On my very first trip to France many years ago I attended a performance of Verdi's opera *The Force of Destiny* (1862) in the old Paris Opéra, the one the Phantom was supposed to have inhabited. A full house was enthusiastic about the set designs, based on paintings by Goya, and the conducting of Julius Rudel. At the conclusion of the night, while the tumultuous applause resounded off the glorious Chagall ceiling, I noticed that an elderly patron had left her seat and was walking delicately down the aisle towards the orchestra pit. Arriving at her destination, she gave an approving pat on the shoulder of the surprised maestro before turning on her heels and tottering off. I have been among many warmly applauding audiences over the years, yet I doubt that I will ever again see a response as heartfelt as that old lady's pat of gratitude.

We won't linger too much over joy. Chabrier aside, it is obviously a state that most composers find less interesting than explorations of the darker emotions.

In opera the most boring parts occur when characters tell us how happy they are; fortunately, their bliss never lasts long.

INTERVAL

We've been feeling pretty good in this narrative so far. Our emotional graph has described an upward spike into the excess zone, granted, but moderation is rarely practised early in a love affair.

Let us practise some here by pausing at the midpoint of the programme, turning up the lights and making our way to the bar for some conviviality and light refreshments. The lessons in love distilled here are not enough for a safe conduct through life. We must take time out from all this passion for some practical advice on things outside love, based again upon our friends' cock-ups.

Enjoy your drink. In the drama of romance, just like an opera, things get darker in the second half.

SOME MUSICAL LIFE TIPS

'The purpose of writing music? Simply a way to wake up to the very life we're living.'

John Cage, 1957

1. DON'T WASTE A MOMENT

It's tempting to imagine composers tinkering endlessly over their operas and symphonies. All that detail takes some fine-tuning. And all those notes! Leonardo da Vinci applied those never-quite-finishing touches to his diminutive *Mona Lisa* for nearly fifteen years. Surely an immense construct like Handel's *Messiah* must have demanded a similar feat of endurance?

Well, no. Apparently it is easier to paint Jesus in sound

than to paint a smile. In 1741 Handel composed *Messiah* end-to-end between 22 August and 14 September, just under three and a half weeks. He slowed to a canter with his next oratorio, *Samson*, which emerged from labour six weeks later on 29 October. Both occupy a very full evening in the hearing. I remember playing a four-minute chorus from his oratorio *Israel in Egypt* (the whole of which found its way to paper in just under the month of October 1738) and remarking that this elaborate piece probably took up most of a day's work, right down to the viola's last semiquaver. One of Handel's librettists, the Reverend Thomas Morell, might well have claimed a miracle had taken place when he delivered the text for an aria, ducked out of the room for a twinkle and returned three minutes later to find that Handel had already completed the vocal line.

Mozart was not only just as fast but could apparently do other things at the same time. In a twist on the ventriloquist who drinks water while his dummy talks, he wrote the overture to his opera *Don Giovanni* while quaffing punch and chatting with his wife the night before the opera's premiere in 1787. Next time you're browsing online at a site like imslp.org have a look at the overture in full score. It would take an ordinary human being more than a night just to copy it out. Mozart's hand is faster than our eye.

The Italian composers of so-called *bel canto* in the early 1800s were the fastest *baristas* of music espresso. The opera world of those days was fast and loose with new pieces churning through provincial houses at an incredible rate. Composers would receive commissions a handful of weeks before opening night. A flop with the audience was met by an Italianate shrug of the shoulders; there was always another new piece due for performance in a month.

Rossini's *The Barber of Seville* occupied him for just thirteen days in 1816, although sections of it (including its overture) were merely recycled from earlier failures. No sense in letting an audience's disapproval kill good material, after all. Rossini's compatriot Gaetano Donizetti knocked off his comedy classic *The Elixir of Love* (1832) in eight days.

Other composers were happier to substitute one big operatic egg with many smaller ones. Songs, for instance. Franz Schubert, Robert Schumann and Hugo Wolf, three of the greatest composers of German song (or *lieder*) in the nineteenth century, were like pigs in gravy if they could set several texts a *day*. I now feel decidedly uncomfortable about the speed at which I have written this book. Do me a favour and read quickly.

2. Never Neglect Home Security

This is even more essential when the immediate family is keen to hasten your demise. The great French violinist and composer Jean-Marie Leclair (1697–1764) fell upon hard domestic times late in life when he parted from his wife and set up in his own small house in one of Paris' less salubrious suburbs. One night he was stabbed to death on his own doorstep. In a scenario Agatha Christie would have loved, the *gendarmerie* settled on three suspects: the gardener, Leclair's wife, and his rival violinist nephew. Most evidence pointed to the last-mentioned but the case was never brought to trial.

3. Classical Music Is a Young Person's Game

Life may be faster now but it was shorter then. Even though demographic research tells us that people tend to come to classical music later in life it would be a mistake to extrapolate a presumption that it is exclusively the domain of seniors. That is what rock music is for; just ask The Rolling Stones. There's nothing wrong with getting on a bit (in fact, I've recently taken to it myself) but it is amusing to note that some of today's time-tested purveyors of musical youth culture are now older than many of my own pin-ups ever were.

The life spans of composers, while not always unusual for the times in which they lived, make exasperating reading today:

Schubert, 31
Mozart, 35
Bizet, 36
Mendelssohn and Gershwin, 38
Chopin, 39

It gets worse. The obviously frail Italian Giovanni Pergolesi, one of the most successful composers of the eighteenth century, made it to twenty-six before his death in 1736, and the exciting new talent for the nineteenth century, Spaniard Juan Crisóstomo Arriaga, died just before his twentieth birthday (1806–1826).

Those who did kick on did so with notoriety acquired early. Our old friend Igor Stravinsky wrote his punkish picture of a young girl dancing herself to death in one of the watershed works of the twentieth century, *The Rite of Spring* (1913), at the age of thirty. Berlioz's swirling musical vortex of lovelorn hallucinations, the *Fantastic Symphony*, bled onto the page when he was twenty-six. Hardly a crow's foot among them, yet we still feel that maturity is the passport to their world.

4. It Is Never Too Late To Begin

Those were some shooting stars; others made a more

languid departure from the starter's box. Tchaikovsky (see *Sadness*) was twenty-one when he began a serious music education; the Frenchman Ernest Chausson (1855–1899) shopped around in writing and drawing, even taking a law degree, before starting formal tuition in music at the age of twenty-four. Erik Satie decided that piano-playing in smoky Parisian cafés wasn't enough training and went back to music school at the age of thirty-nine. *Your* speed is always the right speed.

5. Avoid Public Transport

Music history would suggest that the past catches up with one in quite unexpected ways. Composer Isaac Nathan (1790–1864) enjoyed a good run of removing himself from sticky situations – usually financial ones. Creditors drove him from his native England into Wales in his late twenties. It is possible he was a secret agent for George IV, masquerading as the King's music librarian, a sort of early nineteenth-century James Bond with crotchets.

Consorting with the aristocracy must have earned him a few confidences given that his most conspicuous London operatic stage success was the 1823 *Sweethearts and Wives*. Eventually he was ruined through 'unspecified services' for William IV and emigrated to Australia in

1841, where he became the uncrowned king of the Sydney colonial musical scene: composing, teaching, annotating Aboriginal music, and writing about everything from the arts to boxing. His days of courtly espionage behind him, Nathan penned the alarmingly titled *Merry Freaks in Troublous Time*s (1843); one presumes that casting difficulties prevented a complete production. I feel sure we could surmount those problems today.

Isaac Nathan didn't watch his step and met his accidental end under the wheels of a horse-drawn tram in 1864.

6. Drive Carefully

Puccini and Ravel managed to have nasty accidents even in cars proceeding at a slow speed. The unfortunate Chausson mentioned above, having started late, proceeded to finish early when he fell off his pushbike aged forty-four.

7. Auto-Didacticism Is Good

Today's big hard world is awash with graduates; a person without their validating piece of paper is about as useful as mere air on a G-string. The same holds true for aspiring 'serious' composers. Their armoury of technical knowledge has to be so comprehensive that it can be front-end loaded only in university lecture rooms. Young composers come complete with their papers, rather like hopeful émigrés at a border crossing, or a pedigree spaniel.

To this our musical faces of the past say: have faith in your own powers and the refining crucible of life. I can suggest no motivational techniques save that of comparison, for most great composers of the past never emerged from a classroom with that degree in hand. Some were almost entirely self-taught.

Our friend Georg Philipp Telemann was more celebrated and successful than his contemporary J.S. Bach during their lifetimes. A pastor's son, he is said as a boy to have learned to play the flute, violin and zither before he could read a note. He soon taught himself notation and acquired style by studying the scores of others. I should say *styles*: because Telemann became so technically proficient that he could switch around and write in the German, French or Italian fashions of the day. He picked up music as a child picks up language.

Richard Wagner is perhaps the most breathtaking example of a composer who made his own way. A late starter in music and thereafter a poor performer at school once the mania had bitten him, Wagner scraped a couple of years of lessons from a Leipzig local when in his late teens. The rest of the time was spent alone making his own way through music textbooks, or (more importantly) copying out the music of his musical hero, Beethoven.

Jacques Offenbach (1819–1880) put the crotchets into the can-can – yes, that's his tune – and supplied the heady musical champagne for mid-nineteenth-century France with operettas such as *Orpheus in the Underworld* (1858). You could credit him as the pioneer of what became the twentieth-century musical. And yet this classic Gallic entertainer was born in Germany, the son of a cantor, only going to Paris in search of formal tuition when he was fourteen. His studies at the Paris Conservatoire lasted just a year. Knocking around in the pit orchestras of local theatres proved a greater schooling for the teenage cellist.

Edward Elgar (1857–1934) found himself as a composer only in his forties (see *Sadness*). He taught himself the violin and composition within the congenial surroundings of the family music-shop, receiving his best practical experience conducting the band in a local lunatic asylum. Slow and steady wins, they say; when he finally hit his mother lode it yielded symphonies, concertos and a wealth of incidental music that is still under-estimated outside his native England.

Learning on the job was the reality for the Brazilian Heitor Villa-Lobos (1887–1959) who picked up some tips about the cello from his civil servant father before the latter's death when Heitor was only ten. From then on he was a working musician, busking in the streets of Rio, playing with theatre companies and doing the rounds of cafés. He made some trips into the jungles of the Brazilian interior to suss out the indigenous music there, eventually enrolling at Rio's National Music Institute. By then it was too late for such rigour; he lasted in the lecture-rooms for only a year and then went back to his lonesome road. He does a great impression in *The Little Train of the Caipira*, a shunting, whistling, wheezing vignette from his series called the *Bachianas brasileiras* in which Bach meets Brazil.

An honourable mention goes to a self-taught Dane of whom I'm very fond, Peter Erasmus Lange-Müller (1850–1926), who was spared the drudgery of a professional working life by inherited wealth and could tinker away at his music on a country estate.

8. Just Do It

Many years ago I was obsessed with the ambition of conducting orchestras, and decamped to London just after my nineteenth birthday to observe my heroes at work. Prevailing upon the English maestro Raymond Leppard to let me watch a rehearsal, I asked him afterwards for advice on making a career with the baton.

'If you want to conduct,' he said, 'then conduct.'

In the silence that followed I realised that he was not going to recommend a course of study, a great conservatorium or even a stick-wielding guru. Just go and do it? I thought this a great recipe for charlatanism. Sure enough, there were moments in later years as I sat in recording control booths, watching people self-immolate on the podium, when I wondered if too many had been keen to take Leppard's advice.

He's right, though; the process demands the development of a range of skills besides sheer musicality, and nobler qualities than a liking for telling others what to do (as opposed to real leadership). There *are* snake-oil salespeople in the profession, but there are other maestros who seem to have materialised out of thin air with their astonishing ability, stepping down from the organ loft (like Leopold Stokowski) or up from the orchestra's cello section (like Arturo Toscanini).

This pair emerged more than a century ago, before conductor courses or motivational weekends. Were they running on five-year plans or constant visualisation? Yes – in a sense. Conductors sign multi-year contracts so their working future is always structured for the medium-term, and they need to have an ideal performance of a symphony resonating in their heads before giving the first downbeat. In the end, good old passion is their fuel, and it certainly agrees with them. While music history is brimful of short-lived composers, it's also chockers with maestro Methuselahs. Maybe conductors really do feed on the vital energies that soon-depleted composers have to spill, or maybe it's that aerobic arm waving.

9. Always Choose Built-Ins

Charles Alkan (1813–1888) was a recluse. The French pianist–composer was so crippled by shyness that he gave only six recitals in the space of thirty-five years. He vanished from public view in between engagements and kept to himself, leaving no record of large parts of his life. He dressed like a cleric, and matched his demeanour with the assembly of a large theological library kept in freestanding bookcases, one of which fell over and crushed him to death.

10. It's Okay To Worry About Your Pimples

Described by Aldous Huxley as 'the voluptuous dentist', it seems that the Russian pianist–composer Alexander Scriabin (1872–1915) should have been more careful in the oral hygiene department. He was probably born eighty years too early; his ideas about attaining ecstasy through 'global consciousness' and 'cosmic regeneration' would probably have won him a few adherents in a 1970s California compound, while his attempts at a complete synthesis of music, colour and image might have been achieved with the help of a Stanley Kubrick. Scriabin sported an exquisitely turned moustache, but there was trouble brewing under that facial hair. An unattended pimple grew into full-blown septicaemia that killed him at the age of forty-three.

11. Oranges Are Dangerous . . .

Years ago I played an urchin in a production of the Czech operatic comedy *The Bartered Bride* by Bedrich Smetana (1824–1884). Our stage had limited wing space and the chorus of happy Bohemian peasants had been given no dressing rooms. They resorted to making their costume changes on stage behind the 'flat', or propped-up façade, of the village inn. The vigorous playing of the large student orchestra in the pit masked the sound of mysterious rustling before the next crowd scene.

The liveliest part of the show was the *Dance of the Comedians*, a rollicking folk-ballet complete with spinning couples, a walking bear and a juggler of oranges. To make way for this entourage, the chorus graciously retired to the inn for a quick change into festive garb. The juggler led on the dancers and suffered one of those unfortunate nervous slips of the hand, showering the stage in a citrus cascade. One by one, the oranges rolled forward into the pit, bombing the surprised players and breaking a viola. Our orchestra whirred on and the stage was now full of urchins and dancing peasants. I watched in morbid fascination as the cloud of feet moved inexorably towards the single remaining orange glowing like a traffic light. It happened, of course; a slip, a sudden lurch backward into the delicately poised inn, and with an almighty crash the audience was treated to a time-travel image of nineteenth-century village maidens clutching their 1970s brassieres.

The curtain was brought down on the flattened square amid the uproar and the inn hastily resurrected. There are many stories about the audience pelting the stage with fruit; this is the only instance I know of an attempt in the opposite direction.

12. . . . So Are Mushrooms

Johann Schobert (c1735–1767), not to be confused with Franz Schubert, was admired and imitated by the young Mozart. Thank heavens Wolfgang didn't follow in the older man's culinary footsteps. A promising career was cut short when the composer picked and cooked some wild mushrooms against the advice of a local Parisian tavern-keeper. The poisoned lunch carried away Schobert, together with his wife and child. *Always listen to the locals*.

13. Know When To Fold Them

Death is usually the reason for the end of a composer's career, although many composers have had periods of fallowness; for some, inactivity merged into retirement. The American Charles Ives (1874–1954) wrote music only when he wasn't making a fortune running his own insurance company. One day in 1926, tinkering upstairs in his house with crotchets much as other men might be out with the spare parts in the shed, he came downstairs with tears in his eyes and said that he couldn't compose anymore. The creative spark had gone, just like that. The world's discovery of Ives as a pioneering figure in music happened after this, when his music won the Pulitzer Prize in 1947. But not a single new note could be coaxed from him. (One day, try out his 1906 piece for small orchestra called *The Unanswered Question*.) Ives got on with his life and didn't waste his time mourning the shutdown.

Have you often felt that the times have passed you by, that somehow, just by staying true to yourself, you have dropped out of the loop? At the end of the First World War, the Finn Jean Sibelius (1865–1957), whose symphonies eerily evoke the chill, sparse landscapes of his homeland, was considered one of the major European musical figures, but just a few years later the signposts of his old musical world were being torn out. Nobody was writing the sort of music he liked anymore. Not that he had stayed the same either; his last big orchestral work, *Tapiola* (1926) – which you'll need to listen to in an overcoat, such is the blast of icy wind from the music – feels like the stylistic last stop on the Sibelius line. Perhaps he felt: what else could I do? And the answer, a brave one, was nothing. He put down his pen and lived on for thirty more years, increasingly venerated as the world buzzed with rumour about another symphony that never materialised.

14. Never Be Too Emphatic

The Italian-born Jean Baptiste Lully (1632–1687) was very used to having his own way. He ruled the musical roost at the palace of Versailles and was a favourite of Louis XIV, who occasionally liked to dance onstage in some of his composer's productions. One day Lully was conducting a new *Te Deum* setting to celebrate the King's recovery from an illness. The slender white baton of today and the modern maestro who waves it did not exist in Lully's day; one simply beat time by pounding a wooden staff on the floor, as Gérard Depardieu does in the film *Tous les matins du monde*.

In a moment of excessive zeal, Lully rammed the staff through his foot and fell from the stage. The injury became gangrenous and killed him. Moral: the mighty can be impaled on their own authority.

15. You've Heard It All Before For Good Reason

This reminiscence comes from a motorised pilgrimage through northern Spain described in the *Freedom and Release* chapter. These were splendid days of silence, for I resisted the temptation to be kept company by Spanish talkback radio, feeling that all the incomprehensible gabbling would clutter the surprising emptiness of that part of the country. Several times I reached for the tuning dial on the radio to begin a search for whatever northern Spain had to offer as a classical music station, before returning trembling fingers to the steering wheel. Little did I realise that I was inducing some form of musical malnutrition.

It was a warm May afternoon and lunch was in order. I stopped in a small town near Burgos that seemed unnaturally quiet; siesta was underway. The single open establishment looked strangely salubrious in this rustic setting, a chicken pecking about in sight of its elegant windows. Inside the old stone walls were large cloth-topped tables, set with military precision, and those over-starched serviettes one needs to prise apart with a jemmy, all testifying to a serious attitude. I would be the only guest; a sensation that might have left me feeling self-conscious were it not to help maintain the demeanour of the solitary pilgrim.

A young woman came over to present the menu and I ordered the wrong meal in a language unknown to both of us. Settling back, I noticed the sound system was operating at a discreet whisper – a wonderful development in itself and well worth emulating by any restaurant if they must insist on having any music at all – and that the music was Vivaldi's cycle of violin concertos, *The Four Seasons*.

This ambush disarmed me; my faculty for disregarding music too familiar was suspended. I reheard the music with rapt attention, letting it rain and shine all over my table. This really is very good, I thought. The clarity of texture, the assurance of the writing, the vividness of the swooping strings, the pictures of barking dogs, hunting horns, savage winds and slippery ice made me captive to Vivaldi's imagination. The music's beauty was shameless and generous. I was overwhelmed by the fact that the asthmatic 'Red Priest' of Venice could make me feel so good, so *thankful*, three centuries after his death.

Get a handle on yourself, cautioned the Anglo-Saxon inside. You're starting to lose it. This was true; I was actually shedding a tear in a deserted Spanish restaurant because of the music on the sound system. The chrome-strength serviette couldn't help me now. I dabbed at my face with one sleeve under cover of the menu that curled back rather inconveniently to reveal my travail to the waitress as she approached with a bread roll. No questions asked, she showed concern for the integrity of the just-baked crust by depositing it at some distance from the moistening grasp of my fingers.

I have no recollection of the food after all these years, but I will never forget the rush of that epiphany, an unexpected reminder of music's power to trigger emotion and what a completely intuitive process listening should be. It also reminded me of how much I love the stuff, even the stuff that is hackneyed for some people. Hearing anything for the fiftieth time seems to promote a sense of disengagement (as any teenager will demonstrate) but great music becomes familiar for reasons other than the whim of fashion; it sometimes takes an unexpected hearing to reveal its quality all over again.

I'm all in favour of so-called orchestral 'pops' concerts with Rossini's *William Tell* Overture, Grieg's Piano Concerto, Beethoven's Fifth and Tchaikovsky's *1812*. The music is still fabulous and audiences look sated and excited as they leave. This is music's Sunday roast: comfort food that is always good for you. You can be adventurous again on Monday.

16. Always Carry A Swiss Army Knife

Another restaurant tale: I was touring with a British pianist many years ago, recording some of his recitals along the way for radio broadcasts. Our lunchtime restaurant visit in a country town was marred by the imposition of some ghastly muzak that was doubtless intended to provide 'ambience'. Our polite request to turn it off (we were the only customers) was interpreted as a slur on the good taste of management and the intruding noise was instead turned *up*.

The pianist mentioned that he was prepared for such occasions and loudly excused himself to go to the lavatory. During his brief absence the aural scabies disappeared as if by magic, causing the puzzled staff to begin tapping on the side panel of a troublesome amplifier. The real cause was more sinister; the returning pianist flashed me a glimpse of his Swiss Army knife, and with a tilt of his head indicated the imperceptibly severed speaker cables snaking up the wall.

17. Know When It Is Acceptable To Talk To Strangers

This same pianist claimed to perform certain pieces under the direct supervision of the spirit of the dead composer, so that his recitals were a public display of possession. I took this claim with a grain of salt until deciding to make an interval visit to his dressing room to offer the customary words of encouragement.

There was no response to my knocking on his unlocked door. When I eased it open rather gingerly, I found him alone, holding the music of Liszt's *Transcendental Studies* on his lap, pointing at certain bars while gazing into midair, asking 'What would you like me to do here?' and then pausing for the inaudible reply. I crept away from this one-sided conversation, thoroughly spooked, and realising this was a consultation one shouldn't interrupt. He played with great authority in the second half.

Not long after this a listener to my radio program tracked me down to make an urgent confession, telling me that she had received approval to do so from certain 'advisers'. She was a perfectly lucid middle-aged woman with two adolescent sons and a husband who put in too many hours at a refrigeration company. She had known nothing about music, and had been understandably disconcerted when, while writing a letter to her father several years before, her pen had traced out the phrase 'I am Ludwig van Beethoven'.

After making investigations about the identity of her invisible penpal she resigned herself to his increasingly frequent visits; in fact, she felt a strong attraction to him. Their discussions through the medium of the pen became more intimate. Beethoven was upsetting her marriage. He introduced her to some of his otherworld colleagues and she began forming new friendships. Schubert was a wonderful shopping companion, she said. There was an embarrassing luncheon at which some of her girlfriends began to talk disparagingly about homosexuality, little realising that Tchaikovsky was sitting at their table.

It was Beethoven who was closest to her and eventually he made suggestions as to which recordings of his works she should buy. As she said, he seemed such a lovely person that she wanted to acquaint herself with his music. The Seventh Symphony was a favourite of hers. The composer recommended Karajan over Bernstein. Who was she to quibble? Their dialogue up to this point had been expressed solely via the pen. Once, and only once, did she experience a visual manifestation. The sight of his 'lovely' face was the clincher. She decided to run away with him. Nevertheless, she was uncertain about how news of this unorthodox relationship would be received by her friends. I had been sought out for counsel; what should she do?

I responded that one had to look at past form, and on that basis the signs for the future weren't encouraging (see *Anger*). Sure, Beethoven had probably resolved some personal problems in his new plane of existence. The deafness was certainly no longer an impediment. But the composer had a history of being attracted to married women while being very judgemental about other people's morality; moreover, his real mistress would always be his work. It would be no fun being elbowed aside to make room for a sonata. Far safer, I said, to put this down to experience and opt for friendship. He may not have her body, but there would always be the handwriting.

The advice was accepted and acted upon; when we next spoke, she and Ludwig had worked it out. When I flew out of that city, she met me at the airport and pressed into my hands a small sheaf of envelopes containing letters from her 'circle', Beethoven included. I was instructed to open them only when I was airborne, and to never divulge their contents to anyone.

And I never have.

ANGER

'This is Tosca's kiss!'
>Floria Tosca stabbing to death the evil Baron Scarpia in Puccini's 1900 opera

I've never met anyone who hasn't confessed to getting a bit shirty now and then. Perhaps anger even contributes to the 'flavour' of our personalities, like the infusion from the dregs in a bottle of champagne. No dregs make a dreary drop.

It might be drawing a long bow to try and isolate anger in music, but there are certain works that resonate perfectly with the projected anger of the listener. On tetchy days I might take refuge in Beethoven's *Egmont Overture*, for instance. I'm not a fighter, but it is therapeutic to hear an orchestra give the music a good thumping as invited by the score. It is certainly better than throwing a *papier-mâché* brick at the television. Sometimes, not often, I can understand why certain testosterone-riddled drivers turn their vehicles into boom boxes.

For this is the great surprise about classical music: it is not a sedative. It does not engage us by dulling our reactions. It *does* perform the useful function of opening the windows on certain parts of ourselves and allowing us to observe them one at a time.

But frequently the view is not so good. Why should it be? As you are discovering, composers were usually not serene. One could make the pat suggestion that they were all carrying repressed anger. It had to come out somewhere, and a sheet of empty manuscript paper must have been a tantalising target. You can't be arrested for assaulting your own symphony. Things do get a little hotter, though, when we suspect the music is assaulting *us* (see below).

While listening to and engaging with good music can be a useful catharsis, that doesn't necessarily lead us to the conclusion that it makes us into better people. Don't ever accept the inference from a musical snob that they are a more highly developed being because they 'understand' Bach or Stockhausen, and you don't. Conversely, maintain your composure when an idiot condemns the Stockhausen or Bach they haven't yet understood. At the very least, try not to kick them.

The demolition of the notion of classical music as 'ennobling' was effected forcibly by Stanley Kubrick's 1971 film *A Clockwork Orange*, based on the novel by Anthony Burgess. The portrayal of 'ultra-violence' gave it a notoriety that continues to this day. Even more confronting was the use of Beethoven's music ('lovely Ludwig van') as an aural incitement for the principal gang-leader's violent fantasies and rampages. This raised the prospect that, somehow, good music could also be bad for you.

In the end, music's effect is up to the listener. I feel confident in predicting Beethoven's Ninth Symphony won't turn you into a psychopath. There were no scuffles at the drinks bar during intermission at a performance I attended recently. But Beethoven remains one of the supreme figures in Western music nearly two hundred years after his death because his music's power reaches deep down into the dregs of our bottle.

'I will seize Fate by the throat.'
Ludwig van Beethoven, 1801

And in the red corner, there he is: shortish (165 cm), pugnacious, carrying quite a gut at the weigh-in and doing a great job of filling his ringside spittoon. His opponent in the dark corner, the trim but diaphanous spectre of Fate, is looking shaky after delivering some nasty but effective blows to the composer's ears in the early rounds. The Blaster from Bonn has bounced back from the ropes with the gloves off and has had the unbeaten champion on the mat for the greater part of this fight.

Like all great fighters, Beethoven is driven by anger. You can see it in his portraits, particularly as he gets older; that 'I'm as mad as Hell' look in the eyes, the rebellious hair. You can feel it in his music, emphatic as a fist slamming the table. It's the anger we all feel at some point in our lives over our unfair treatment at the hands of Fate.

I'm not talking about petty irritations here, although Beethoven could blow a gasket over those too, as in his 1795 piano piece *Rage over a Lost Penny*. No – this is the big one. Everyone cheers for Ludwig in this supreme contest because he's up there slugging it out for all of us.

Some philosophies and religions espouse a more passive response to some of life's low blows. We're supposed to just take the punches and let the bad moment pass. This was not Beethoven's way. He would never go gently into anyone's good night.

You know how the bout ends, of course. Fate wins the struggle through sheer endurance. But Beethoven would keep an uppercut in reserve right through to the end in 1827; it is said that on his deathbed he shook his fist in defiance at a thunderclap as a storm raged outside.

~

Beethoven is an essential but nevertheless difficult life guide in a book such as this. Being 'guided' at all presupposes an element of cooperation, a degree of bending with the wind. Ludwig fully expected the world to bend to *him*, which made for a great musical outcome with a few rude shocks in life's other departments. The difficulty in appearing to be flippant about Beethoven is a measure of our respect for his achievement, and shows the extent to which he has been mythologised by succeeding generations of composers and audiences.

The modern notion of the artist is still modelled after Beethoven's example. Indeed, he was one of the first to describe himself as an 'artist'. You know the image: the wild-haired dysfunctional rebel, cocking a snook at the old ways of thinking and behaviour, a loose cannon at social gatherings, unkempt and unhygienic, creating world-shattering fancies in an isolated garret.

The image has been building up since before Beethoven's death, but we still cherish it as an effective role model for several generations of rock musicians, all frowning and venting their spleen in video clips. To be an angry young man or woman in contemporary arts is to be perceived as violently creative and iconoclastic.

This fashionable discontent, what we call the 'artistic temperament', is a far cry from Beethoven. His was the authentic angst; but let's get things in proportion. Ludwig is of paramount importance *not* because he convinces us that he alone is suffering on a cosmic scale; instead, he reassures us that we're *all* in the basket. What's more, he says, life may be lousy for us, but the situation can be turned around by some healthy lunges at Fate's throat.

Beethoven is classical music's motivational speaker, and the message is uniquely empowering. Orchestras know this. Beethoven festivals with all the symphonies and concertos are still sure-fire crowd pullers. Watch the audience at the end of a Beethoven piece; you might even catch a bit of sympathetic fist pumping from the executives in the crowd who know they're now going to nail that deal in the morning. Tired concertgoers suddenly develop straight backs. They bolt for the trains before the applause ends with a renewed sense of purpose. Not to do so would somehow be letting Beethoven down, because he has generously shown us the power of the individual will in an unsympathetic world.

While Father Bach advises us to stay chilled because it will all come right when you die, Ludwig yells that the time for action is now. He's hunting big game, although the trophies aren't material ones, apart from a decent plate of veal now and then. For him, winners get the preservation of integrity and the natural rule of freedom, all good democratic goals. No guns please, just a good steady forward march – and don't spare the headbutts.

Do we end up being happy? Perhaps that's not the

point, even if Beethoven's Ninth Symphony ends with the world singing an Ode to Joy. Rather, the process, the *living*, is the thing. You've probably read something like this before in various books of Eastern philosophy. It's revelatory to hear it enacted in sound.

The English conductor Sir Thomas Beecham (1879–1961) apparently blamed Beethoven for the 'wrath' later to come in music. The implication from such a remark is that music was quite 'nice' until this unkempt German came along. Much as I admire Beecham, it's what one would expect from someone who probably overdid the *eau de toilette*. Beethoven's music has an almost unprecedented physicality about it, exuding its own sweat; naturally we get an unpleasant whiff now and then. But these metaphysical workouts were often propelled by anger, and as you'll see, he had a lot to work through.

Wouldn't *you* be angry if:

Your childhood was a mess

Ludwig was baptised on 17 December 1770 in Bonn, Germany. His father, a lacklustre tenor at the local court, was a drunkard who both promoted and resented his eldest surviving son's talent. The household was very possibly a violent one. Beethoven also felt that his mother wasn't very affectionate towards him. Sickness may have been the cause; tuberculosis killed her when he was sixteen.

The family fortunes went into rapid decline as his father's drinking increased, jeopardising his employment.

In such a vortex, the eighteen-year-old took charge in 1789, petitioning for half his father's court salary in order to support two younger brothers so that Dad wouldn't otherwise go through it at the local tavern. When Beethoven senior died just three years later, Ludwig didn't so much as mention the fact in his diary.

It is understandable that a highly sensitive person might emerge from such a childhood with 'baggage'. Beethoven would always have problems with authority figures, be they well-meaning teachers like Franz Joseph Haydn (1732–1809), with whom Beethoven studied for a year and then disparaged later in life, or princes (see 3); hardly career-boosting qualities to have at a time when patronage by the aristocracy was still a composer's best chance at a regular meal-ticket. Beethoven would have been a Pandora's Box on any modern psychiatrist's couch, assuming he could have heard the questions, which brings us to:

You're about to make it as a musician and your hearing goes

This is where Fate almost delivers an early knockout. There is Beethoven in the big smoke of 1790s Vienna, beginning to carve out a real name for himself as a pianist capable of astonishing improvisations, if something of a string-breaker. At this stage, he was society's favourite party pianist, playing in the salons of wealthy homes and later making some successful appearances at the newfangled entertainment vehicle of public concerts. His list of students included young Hungarian countesses; he enjoyed the hospitality of the nobility during the summer at their country estates, and publishers were vying for his work (his first couple of piano concertos and early chamber music date from this period). The money was coming in quite nicely. Not yet thirty, he was the Bonn boy made bonny.

Even during these early salad days Beethoven noticed something awry with his hearing. By 1801 his deafness had already become severe enough to make normal social discourse difficult; conversation at parties was next to impossible. The most savage irony was that this decline in the tools of his trade coincided with Beethoven's own awareness of the rapid development of his powers. His depression was overwhelming. In 1802, taking a last-ditch therapeutic break in a village outside Vienna, he penned a long letter to his two brothers that we now know as the 'Heiligenstadt Testament'. Part will, part farewell to life (although rejecting the notion of suicide), it details his personal devastation over his illness: 'as the autumn leaves fall and wither, likewise hope has faded for me.'

The constant droning of tinnitus was a torture for Beethoven over the next dozen years. He was practically stone deaf by 1815, and friends would have to 'talk' to him by writing in conversation books. When the Ninth Symphony was premiered in 1824 the composer was completely unaware of the audience's enthusiastic reception and had to be turned around to acknowledge the applause.

People you consider undeserving end up with the lot

At a time when composers were beginning to work without the crutch of aristocratic largesse, Beethoven was one of the first to declare that mere class was subordinate to talent. He was a standard-bearer by example of the emerging Romantic ideal of the Artist as Hero. Even as the Austrian Prince Karl Lichnowsky offered Beethoven money, encouragement and performance opportunities, the composer could haughtily remind his benefactor in an 1806 letter that 'there are and will be thousands of princes. There is only one Beethoven'.

You have no success with women

Being a hearing-impaired member of the lower classes didn't qualify one as Vienna's Bachelor of the Year where whole pedigrees were at stake; moreover, Beethoven's personality made it impossible for even male friends to live with him. There is no doubt he desperately wanted a life partner; his one opera *Fidelio* (1805) literally sings the praises of conjugal love.

But the women he wanted didn't want him, or were not in a position where they could have him. At least one was already married and the likely recipient of Beethoven's famous 1812 letter to 'the Immortal Beloved' found among his papers after his death. This represents a sad pivotal moment in the composer's life, as it would in anyone's life; the moment when one realises, or decides, that there is no likelihood of fully reciprocated love. Small wonder that Beethoven plunged into depression, writing virtually nothing for years before deciding (as he had in dealing with his deafness) that once again, Art must fill the void. He wrote in his journal in 1816, 'you may be a man no longer ... for you there is no longer happiness except in yourself, in your art'.

Someone you admire lets you down

Beethoven was a great fan of Napoleon and a supporter of the general's campaign for a French Republic. When he began work on his Third Symphony in 1803 it bore the title 'Bonaparte'. This epic work was the longest symphony written up to that time, one that detonates so many musical conventions, exploding out of the frame like the brushwork in many van Gogh paintings.

In May 1804 the diminutive Napoleon gave way to his considerably taller aspirations and proclaimed himself

Emperor. Beethoven was furious at the news; his liberating hero had become just another power-hungry tyrant. He picked up his score of the new Symphony and scratched out the 'Bonaparte' title so violently that his pen tore the paper. It was eventually published as the 'Heroic', or *Eroica* Symphony, written 'in memory of a great man'.

Your brother is shagging his lodger's wife's sister

I suspect there's an element of point 3 in this one. If it isn't happening for you because of life's unfeeling capriciousness, there is plenty of resentment to be harboured if it appears to be happening for someone else. In this case, it turned Beethoven into an interfering prude.

When he heard in 1812 that his younger bachelor brother, Johann, was having some fun between the sheets with a similarly available woman, the composer hurried over to Linz to break up the affair. He ranted to his brother, who presumably told him to mind his own business. Beethoven then went to the local bishop, the civil authorities, and finally to the police station seeking to have the woman thrown out of town. Johann settled the matter by making his mistress his wife. Stung by his brother's 'up yours', Ludwig retreated to Vienna. At this time he was writing his Eighth Symphony, perhaps the most light-hearted of the series.

Restaurant service is lousy

What would you do if you received the wrong plate of food in a restaurant? Accept it anyway, or politely bring it to the waiter's attention and have the dish sent back? Beethoven did neither; when he was erroneously served stewed beef in a Viennese tavern called the 'Swan', the composer picked up his dinner and tipped it over the waiter's head.

You can't be a parent and you're not much of a guardian

Not satisfied with being the brother from Hell, Beethoven proved to be similarly gifted as brother-in-law and uncle when his other brother died suddenly in 1815, leaving a nine-year-old son called Karl. Uncle Ludwig decided that he should be the child's guardian and waged a five-year legal battle with Karl's mother for sole custody, accusing her at various times of embezzlement, prostitution and theft. The welter of slander worked and the matter was finally resolved in Beethoven's favour in 1820.

Here at last was the possibility of a family life that he felt had always been denied him. But a great composer can't be good at everything, and in Ludwig's case one of his lesser skills was surrogate fatherhood. In 1826 nephew Karl fired two pistols at his own head in a botched suicide attempt before being returned to his mother's care.

SWOONING

You want a good drink and all you get is medicine

Even as Beethoven was exploring new musical terrain in his late series of masterpieces – the final piano sonatas, the Ninth Symphony, and the last string quartets – his external life was in increasing disarray. He moved lodgings more than forty times during his Vienna years and was the nemesis of dozens of domestic servants who fell victim to his temper and his preference for squalor; friends sometimes had to change his clothes while he slept.

Under the pressure of such steam, cracks were bound to appear, and they did: Beethoven drank so much that by his early fifties his liver began to fail. He died on 26 March 1827 from cirrhosis. In his final weeks he was overjoyed when one of the attending doctors prescribed an alcoholic iced punch as a sleeping aid. Beethoven took to the medicine with such vigour that it hastened his end.

∼

That is just a little of Beethoven's story. Like any distillation of the bad moments inside fifty-six years it is bound to make grim reading; much more so than the petty irritations we all endure and which often suffice to stop most of us in our tracks. It is natural to think that gaining speed on that distant carrot of life's purpose is impossible when so many small obstacles keep interrupting our stride. They remind us that ours is an ordinary life.

The extraordinary being that was Beethoven would have found some of the creature comforts of 'ordinariness', a Biedermeier postcard existence, to have been reassuring. Instead, his output petered away to nothing for years at a time while he was overwhelmed by depression or the thought-sapping minutiae of daily life: his legal wrangling over custody of his nephew, for instance. Crowning it all was his sense of being an outsider, an ostracism imposed by deafness, and probably a tremendous loneliness. Seen from the outside, he didn't cope too well. No wonder he wanted to get his hands on Fate's throat.

Every life is ordinary in the sense that we all receive low blows from the shadowy bastard across the ring. Following Beethoven's suggested tactic of going at the opponent doesn't guarantee victory, however; his particular advantage was in using his music as a blunt instrument to force his way through to some universal truth. His musical sketchbooks carry the scars of the battle. Much of his work didn't flow onto the page in finished form, but was chiselled into final form through the discarding, refinement, crossing-out, and reworking of ideas. We think we know what we want, but getting to the right solution needs agonising work. If anything is superhuman about Beethoven, it is this sense of effort.

There is a lot to learn from the sight of Beethoven wrestling with his initial ideas. Even if we think we know initially what we want, getting to the right solution requires agonising and relentless work. Self-observation is a useful tool here in having a good dialogue with oneself. This is the disciplined process of the creative artist enacted within the mundane reality of sitting alone, converting thoughts into symbols on paper or a computer screen. Composition is like life: a journey to the interior, asking directions on the way.

If the going gets rough and you feel angry about life's apparent injustice, listen to Beethoven's *Eroica* Symphony, the massive work he wrote after the Heiligenstadt Testament, when he had to try and accept his encroaching deafness as a permanent state and push on with the business of life regardless. The symphony doesn't just start; it *detonates* with a couple of monumental uppercuts that turn the contest around in our favour in the existential slugfest. His music abounds with these killer blows, such as the first movement of his *Pathétique* piano sonata, Op.13 (1799), the end of the *Egmont* Overture, the opening of the final movement of the Ninth Symphony. You will feel positively empowered.

ANGER

Losing It

Wagner said with characteristic bluntness, 'I am not made like other people.' Certainly he became the avatar of so-called 'artistic' temperament: bad behaviour, temper tantrums, demanding one's own way, stamping of the feet. By this definition, many three-year-olds are artistic. They may be great musicians, but would you really want to know some people like these?

The most famous maestro of all, Arturo Toscanini (1867–1957) achieved astonishing results through a reign of terror, culminating in his dictatorship of the NBC Symphony Orchestra in the US. The players would watch in horror as his foot-stamping fits of disapproval routinely crushed spectacles, batons and fob watches. Eventually they gave him a watch in a solid iron casing inscribed 'For Rehearsals'. Toscanini once became so incensed with an unresponsive soprano that he rushed onstage, grabbed her reportedly spectacular breasts and screamed 'if only these were brains!'

Orchestras can turn the tables. Moments before a performance, the Turin Opera Orchestra ambushed its conductor and management with a refusal to play unless fee demands were met. Calling the players' bluff, the conductor Peter Maag went onstage, explained the situation to the restive audience and declared that he would play the accompaniment on a piano instead. The night was a triumph and the orchestra went home in disgrace.

The eighteenth-century Italian composer and violin virtuoso Francesco Veracini was considered in his day to be a little on the wild side. In 1722 Veracini jumped from a third-storey window in a fit of pique. The limping composer later claimed that there had been a plot against his life.

Maria Callas was legendary for her voice and her temper. In 1951 she attacked a Brazilian impresario with a bronze paperweight after he replaced her in a production of Puccini's *Tosca*. In Rome, in 1958, she walked out of a performance of Bellini's *Norma* after the first act due to a rowdy reception; the President of Italy was in the audience.

In 1945 the principal bass with the National Opera of Mexico, Ignacio Ruffino, found himself with spare time during rehearsals and decided to catch a matinée session at the local cinema. Edging his way to his seat, he noticed his wife further along, looking rather too comfortable under the cloak of darkness with his best friend. Realising that discussion was impractical while the film was running, Ruffino pulled out his revolver and shot the man dead instead. As the perpetrator of a crime of passion, the singer was arrested but never tried. Buoyed by the sympathy of Mexican society, Ruffino continued to appear at the Opera and was happily reconciled with his wife.

Hell Hath No Fury

While Giacomo Puccini consistently sent his lead soprano characters to a tragic end in his operas (see *Love*), the most tragic end of all occurred when life imitated art. His own romantic life would have inspired many an opera plot.

In 1884 he eloped with Elvira Gemignani, the wife of a merchant from Puccini's hometown of Lucca. Two years later, though still his mistress, Elvira bore him a son. Their ménage could not be legalised until the death of Elvira's husband in 1904; this was nineteenth-century Catholic Italy.

When the success of his opera *Manon Lescaut* brought Puccini fame and the beginning of riches in 1893, the composer began to succumb frequently to his roving eye and the temptations offered by his new celebrity. Elvira was able to overlook his endless liaisons while they took place away from the Puccini *casa* at Torre del Lago, but her jealousy festered and finally erupted in 1908 when she became convinced that her husband was helping himself to their maid.

The fact that Puccini was wrongly accused in this instance didn't stop the enraged Signora Puccini from persecuting the young Doria Manfredi with such psychological efficiency that the younger woman committed suicide in January 1909. The ensuing court case scandalised Italy, with the complete vindication of the deceased, Puccini paying out a considerable settlement to the girl's family and the sentencing of Elvira to five months in prison.

Puccini's next opera *The Girl of the Golden West* was premiered the following year. It is an American cowboy romance in which the guy ends up with the girl – a rare plot ending for the composer.

~

The Angry Mob

As Puccini put it 'Spectators are good people one by one. But together, once out for evil, they are rabble.' If you are scared of public disapproval, or sometimes doubt your own judgement, then don't become a composer who insists on having your work performed.

While Rossini's opera *The Barber of Seville* has long been one of the genre's favourite comedies, the first performance in 1816 was a disaster. Whistling and hooting drowned out the singing from the start. The composer was hissed as he sat in the orchestra pit. One of the principals accidently fell through an open trapdoor as he sang and a cat walked across the stage during the first finale.

A staging mishap also marred the first night of Puccini's *Madam Butterfly* in 1904 at La Scala in Milan. Butterfly spun around onstage in her kimono too quickly, causing it to billow up over her head, rather like Marilyn Monroe's frock in *The Seven Year Itch*. A member of the audience yelled 'Butterfly is pregnant!' The performance continued amid a welter of obscene remarks and barnyard imitations. There was no applause at the final curtain, only laughter. Puccini hid in a dressing room; afterwards, he left with the conductor's score to preclude a second performance at the house.

The 1913 premiere of Stravinsky's ballet *The Rite of Spring* in Paris is perhaps the most famous first-night fiasco in music history. The hubbub began within seconds of opening and eventually grew to such a pitch that the dancers on stage couldn't hear the pounding of the immense orchestra, and had to listen instead to the counting of the beat yelled from the wings, rather like a coxswain to the rowing team. There was much exchanging of abuse in the stalls; scuffles broke out between people armed with umbrellas. Stravinsky's supporters were just as vocal. Fellow composer Florent Schmitt shouted to the stalls 'Shut up, you bitches!' Stravinsky spent the next few weeks recovering in a nursing home.

Public opinion turned around quickly for all these works. Rossini and Puccini became very wealthy men as their operas were reappraised within weeks. Stravinsky's *Rite* is one of the iconic creations of twentieth century culture, period. He lived long enough to give autographs to Frank Sinatra and the Pope.

SADNESS

'Our sweetest songs are those that tell of saddest thought.'
Percy Bysshe Shelley, *To a Skylark* (1820)

If we agree with Oscar Wilde and Igor Stravinsky that music doesn't represent anything, it follows that, being essentially abstract, music's capacity to incite emotion is reliant on the susceptibility of the listener. In other words, the more one is moved, the more one is a sucker. Two centuries ago the English politician and journalist William Cobbett stated that 'a great fondness for music is a mark of great weakness and great vacuity of mind', a disconcerting assertion for suckers like me whose strongest response to music remains an emotional one.

But whether music 'finds' the emotion or vice versa is difficult to say. Despite some of the recommendations in this book, there remains the probability that no single piece of music is guaranteed to make you happy. This is evidenced by the expression on the faces of orchestral conductors who, after all, know what is coming and never look too pleased about it.

Can music, then, make you sad? I suppose that depends on one's vulnerability at the time: I haven't wept at the sound of an accordion since a long-ago spring afternoon in Paris, although I can still wince over a concertina. The jury has been out on this for centuries, ranging from Cervantes ('he who sings scares away his woes', *Don Quixote*) to Shakespeare ('I am never merry when I hear sweet music', *The Merchant of Venice*). Music has certainly been more than happy to *describe* sadness in all its forms. Melancholy, grief, regret, self-loathing: its tapestry has many black threads.

One would imagine that composers have the misery-peddling franchise all to themselves. In truth, we're about as unhappy as they were; they just look more miserable because smiling was the first casualty of poor dental hygiene (although twentieth-century composers aren't grinners, come to think of it). There *are* exceptions, composers who were especially wired for both a lifetime and an *oeuvre* of sadness. One of the flag-bearers of this tragic troupe is Peter (or to be more Russian about it) Pyotr Ilyich Tchaikovsky (1840–1893).

'Fate hangs perpetually over our heads and is always embittering the soul.'

Pyotr Ilyich Tchaikovsky, 1878

Today, the world loves Tchaikovsky. In his own day he was also popular, even lionised. This celebrity and official recognition didn't help his morale; he was miserable, full of self-loathing and doubts about his work, constantly pessimistic about life's transience. His music often displays a grandiose sense of tragedy, even when it is in a major key. Listen to the opening of the *pas de deux* from his ballet *The Nutcracker* (1892), simply a descending major scale. It's slow, but it should feel happy; church bells sound the same thing as a celebratory peal. In Tchaikovsky's hands the effect is quite the opposite, and the melody moves on with obvious relief to the related minor key.

The opening of the glorious *Serenade for Strings* (1880) is similarly resplendent but again, just a little uncomfortable about it. The pretence of happiness never lasts long. The list of his works includes an early symphonic poem called *Fate*; the *Sérénade mélancolique*; and his final composition, the *Pathétique* Symphony, with its mournful and pessimistic ending. (To be fair to Tchaikovsky, it was his brother who came up with the title, which in Russian connotes something more passionate than 'pathetic'.)

And yet the beauty of the music proves Shelley's poetic

dictum quoted above. What gets us about Peter? Simply this: his are some of the 'sweetest songs' ever written. Tchaikovsky had the knack of having the right tune at the right time. He could even come up with the right tune at the wrong time, such as the opening of his first Piano Concerto, in which that immortal melody is intoned by the orchestra over crashing piano chords, only to be promptly discarded and never referred to again. A brain has to be crammed with ideas to come up with a whopper like that and then just move on because there is so much more to do.

Tchaikovsky often felt compelled by a sense of urgency, of racing against the clock. Even in his mid-forties he would write of life's brevity, of things yet to be accomplished: 'We keep putting things off and meanwhile death lurks round the corner.' He would be depressed about the end of each passing day and eventually kept a number of diaries as a way of making a souvenir of time. When he then became anxious about others seeing their contents, he ensured most of them were destroyed.

∼

One of five sons in a family from a background of military service, there were firm expectations about the direction of Tchaikovsky's career. His father was a successful mining engineer; 'composer' was not the occupation of choice for sons of good middle-class families in mid-nineteenth century Russia. Young Peter would tinker for hours on the family orchestrion (a sort of domestic calliope, the bells and whistles contraption that serenades merry-go-rounds) and he complained about the difficulty of removing music lodged in his head; but every sensitive young kid has fancies.

This calm childhood in the provinces was interrupted in 1848 when Père Tchaikovsky dragged everyone to the big smoke of St Petersburg to pursue a job offer that proved illusory, a move that necessitated the retrenchment of Peter's beloved governess Fanny Dürbach. Unhappy schooldays and a six-month rest spell with measles followed. And then, in 1854, the emotionally fragile teenager was shattered by the death of his mother from cholera.

Music became his consolation. Peter improvised at the piano and made a few stabs at writing with his still rudimentary technical knowledge. After leaving school in 1859 (where his grades had been ordinary) Tchaikovsky became a clerk in the Ministry of Justice, staying there for four years and being the young dandy around town after hours. Not until he was twenty-one did Tchaikovsky begin the serious theoretical study of music. Even Berlioz hadn't left it this late.

It was a long time coming, but when Tchaikovsky eventually found his purpose, an immense and long-dormant creative faculty was activated. This was a man who worried constantly about having enough time left to empty the contents of a mind seething with ideas. Two years after taking up music study full-time he was already teaching harmony at the new Moscow Conservatoire. By 1869 he had written his first masterpiece, the *Romeo and Juliet* Fantasy Overture (complete with one of the great love themes), spurring him into the 1870s and works like the *Marche Slave*, the first Piano Concerto, the Violin Concerto, the Fourth Symphony, his first ballet *Swan Lake*, and the opera *Eugene Onegin*. The musical tap was running.

Meanwhile, other pressures were building. Tchaikovsky was gay, and the ensuing struggle with his sexuality was the great drama of his life. In his time in Russia, homosexuality was an offence punishable by exile to Siberia, but the composer's efforts to suppress this part of himself would appear to have been driven by more complex causes than a fear of suspicion, or worse, conviction; there were always opportunities in big cities like St Petersburg and Moscow. He was a captive of the prevailing morality of the time and felt tremendous guilt about his 'inclinations', which he described in contradictory terms as both 'natural' and 'the greatest obstacle to happiness'.

Tchaikovsky's attempted solution in 1877 was desperate and naive in the extreme. Declaring that marriage would silence rumours about him, he proceeded to wed an unstable young woman who had written him a love letter in which she threatened suicide if he would not see her.

He proposed within a week of their first meeting, knowing full well that a physical relationship would be impossible.

Oh, Peter. He probably said the same early on their honeymoon night on the train from Moscow to St Petersburg. (Ken Russell's film about Tchaikovsky, *The Music Lovers*, offers a graphic representation of the naked and optimistic Mrs Tchaikovsky rolling around the floor of their compartment. In reality, the composer was 'on the point of screaming', while his wife stayed obligingly clothed and upright.) The arrangement was an instant catastrophe; Tchaikovsky was on the verge of a complete breakdown within days. In early October he tried to induce pneumonia by walking into the freezing Moskva River, and fled from Moscow days later to suffer a complete nervous collapse while under the care of one of his younger brothers. Doctors recommended that he never see his wife again; this astute prescription initiated a swift recovery. The former Mrs Tchaikovsky was certified as insane in 1896 and died in an asylum in 1917.

Concurrent with Tchaikovsky's marital fiasco ran another relationship with a woman that maintained a higher degree of candour and emotional intimacy than found in many marriages. It was conducted entirely by mail with one Nadezhda von Meck, the wealthy widow of a railway magnate. Her admiration for the composer had more than a touch of love in it and was manifested in a generous annuity that helped to keep him afloat financially for fourteen years (1876–1890), partially subsidising the composition of great works like the Fourth and Fifth Symphonies (he dedicated the first of these to her), the *Serenade for Strings* and the *Capriccio Italien*. She was his long-distance shoulder to cry on – meaning that her shoulder was perpetually moist – and invisible hostess at several estates where Tchaikovsky could work and weep alone, rent-free. Apart from accidental sightings on two occasions, the pair never met.

~

The composer was restless when at home and homesick while away. In the years immediately after his marriage he travelled extensively around Europe with generous financial assistance from supporters at the Russian Musical Society, from his benefactress Nadezhda von Meck, and eventually from the Tsar himself. He was free to compose full-time, but this liberty brought him little joy because of his ruthless self-criticism. 'I have achieved nothing,' he would write, 'am I played out?' For many years alcohol was his comfort.

Concert tours took him as far afield as the United States, where he conducted in the opening concerts at Carnegie Hall in 1891. (He had become more secure on the podium since his first-ever appearance in 1868, when he was terrified that his head would fall off.) Tchaikovsky's sister died before the tour began, so the devastated composer spent his first night in New York weeping in his hotel room.

His constant depressions made him hypochondriacal; he complained of insomnia, 'apoplectic strokes', migraines and various aches and pains. 'You cannot imagine anyone who suffers more than I do', he wrote to his brother Modest in 1874. He would assert that the compulsion to feign illness was as much an illness as any actual physical infirmity.

We shouldn't imagine that Tchaikovsky composed by shedding copious tears on a blank page, watching them blossom into crotchets. The dialogue with himself achieved by writing music gave him his greatest happiness; it is a common observation from study of the lives of these composers that creative hard work can be therapeutic. Sure, these artists may have been a bit AWOL once the pen, the brush or the chisel was put down – the odd fired pistol, sliced ear or (in Tchaikovsky's case) spilled vodka – but the process of organising and notating thought in a work as complex as, say, his *Pathétique* Symphony requires absolute clarity of mind. You can't meander drunkenly through a fugue.

This symphony is a good example. Tchaikovsky was in appalling spirits before starting the work in February 1893, writing that 'my faith in myself is shattered, and my role is ended'. Then the engine turned over; three weeks later, he had already sketched out the complete first movement on paper with the rest of the piece ready in his head. He realised he still had the ticker. The music collapses with grief at the end of the work, yet it was composed on a high. Tchaikovsky was uncharacteristically upbeat about its quality, declaring the symphony his best and 'most sincere' work. Even the lukewarm reception from the audience and the critics at its premiere in St Petersburg on 28 October didn't faze him.

Just nine days later Tchaikovsky died, aged fifty-three, and here is where rumour and debate step in. His brother Modest maintained that Peter rashly drank a glass of unboiled water and succumbed to cholera, the same disease that had killed his mother. Whether it was accidental or not was unclear, but there was an appealing poetry in thinking that the *Pathétique* was a musical suicide note.

Another equally unverifiable story emerged in 1980, courtesy of a Russian musicologist. This time, Tchaikovsky was going to be 'outed' by a member of the aristocracy in a letter to the Tsar that accused the composer of shenanigans with the complainant's nephew. The letter's emissary, an 'old boy' of the School of Jurisprudence which Tchaikovsky had attended in the 1850s, was disturbed at the disgrace this would bring upon the institution. A strange meeting of other 'old boys' was convened with the composer present. The verdict of this strange jury was that the School's honour must be preserved by his immediate suicide. Arsenic did the job in this scenario.

Evidence is sketchy, so we'll likely never know what happened to this master who died so suddenly at fifty-three, very much at the height of his powers. *Mystery* isn't a chapter this time around, but in classical music's lengthy list of whodunits the Tchaikovsky case is a big one.

FEELING LOW?
Try these Sure-Fire
Tchaikovsky ANTI-DEPRESSANTS!!

Things look grim at the end of the Sixth Symphony – there's help nearby! Just go to the penultimate movement of the same work: a roof-raising march. Go get 'em! it roars. You'll be on your feet and hooting for more after the finale to the Violin Concerto, Op.35. This one's a fighter. Its dedicatee declared it impossible to play, and the reviews were hardly more complimentary after its 1881 premiere: 'music that stinks to the ear', said one. She's come up roses ever since.

Sad Is Interesting

Music has a very simple way of suggesting the 'blues': the so-called 'minor' scale with its flattened third that somehow proposes a darker, sadder, more complex world than the ostensibly happier major scale. Imagine the opening of Mozart's Symphony No. 40 played in G major, rather than G minor; it would sound almost twee. If at the end of a symphony the initial miserable minor scale theme is given a 'major' reincarnation, it denotes a triumphant passage into the light; the challenging process of working things out is over.

In opera, characters only reveal their complexity when they are miserable. A happy diva has less to sing about than one who is contemplating suicide or disgrace. Dido, the Queen of ancient Carthage, sounds pleased when she's being courted by Aeneas in Purcell's *Dido and Aeneas* and Berlioz's *The Trojans*, but it is only after he has dumped her to take an early package tour to Italy that her music becomes truly great; she is literally dying with grief. Unalloyed happiness in opera is usually given to the chorus at beginning of Act One (often tavern scenes or tableaux of simple village life), to the local idiot, or to those in positions of subservience. Such delight displayed by the lower classes must have provided some reassurance to opera's well-heeled patrons.

Sadness in music almost always involves the loss of something once possessed rather than frustrated ambition. There aren't too many operas and symphonies about failing to get a promotion. Lost love, loss of youth and innocence, and plain old being 'lost' are high in the rankings.

Edward Elgar (1857–1934) was deeply affected by loss, subsuming it into nostalgia for a vanishing world, the disappearance of a way of life. There is not a great deal we can do about the 'things aren't what they used to be' misery: hide from a changing world, or endure the flow. But a man who at sixty-four could describe himself as 'still at heart a dreamy child' was not one to embrace life's future possibilities. Even in his mid-forties, when life and career were on the up, Elgar was sentimental about his childhood, writing two little pieces for small orchestra called *Dream Children* (1902), after an essay by Charles Lamb that concludes 'We are nothing; less than nothing, and dreams. We are only what might have been.' This, from a composer with the *Enigma Variations*, the song cycle *Sea Pictures*, and the oratorio *The Dream of Gerontius* – three masterpieces in three years – just behind him.

Elgar was able to capture the national mood of late Victorian and Edwardian England: the opulence, the occasionally blustering pride, the beating of the national heart beneath the bodice. When this too passed, Elgar regretted it; his post-war works have a valedictory quality, like the magnificent Cello Concerto of 1919, and when his much-loved wife, Alice, died in 1920 most of his creative spark went with her. He composed almost nothing more and retreated to the countryside, consoling himself with trips to the races. On his deathbed, he muttered a short remark about himself to a friend that will always remain a secret; 'only five words,' said the friend, 'but they are too tragic for the ear of the mob.' What possible phrase could be so devastating?

Franz Schubert (1797–1828) writes like an old friend, the pudgy scholarly guy in the corner who murmurs words of wisdom in an undertone. I'm tempted to describe him as a sad figure purely on the basis of his short lifespan. We often fancy that those who die young have some subliminal premonition that makes them write at speed in the meantime. It is true that Schubert gushed, rather than composed, hundreds of songs onto paper in his thirty-one years. It is an equally good bet that he would have gushed hundreds more with a few more decades under his belt.

Schubert's friends adored him. He frequented many a Viennese café and played great piano at parties; but despite these good times there is twilight in much of his music, a sense of transience, a real knowledge of the agony of love and the pain of rejection. The mournful narrator of the song cycle *The Fair Maid of the Mill* (1823) experiences all the emotions outlined in this book in the course of an unrequited love, yet his peace comes only when he drowns himself.

The cycle is a symbol of Schubert's own inner turmoil. In 1822 he contracted syphilis from a prostitute, and much of the work was written while he was in hospital receiving ghastly mercury treatments prescribed at the time, causing him to lose some of his hair. It is heart-rending to read a letter by a young man who writes 'I feel myself to be the most unhappy and wretched creature in the world... on retiring to bed, I hope I may not wake again' (1824). But Schubert is a hero and he pushed on – if not with the confidence of before.

The Sorrow Of Parting

Schubert was prey to self-blame, whereas the fatalism of Gustav Mahler (1860–1911) encompasses life and the world. Perhaps he was predisposed to such a philosophy, for even as a child he declared that his life's ambition was to be a martyr. Much later, as a patient of Sigmund Freud's, he recalled that he once ran terrified from his childhood home during a violent argument between his parents, only to hurtle into a street hurdy-gurdy grinding out a popular Viennese song. The memory of this juxtaposition of banality and pain never left him. As the twentieth century trundled by, Mahler's aesthetic resonated ever more profoundly with those who thought of this as a banal, painful, beautiful world.

A Mahler symphony is a trip that takes up most of a concert (there are nine, plus a tenth completed by someone else). One can't help feeling like a psychiatrist while listening to it as Gustav spills the beans from the couch. Even if you're into his confessions, a thermos with warm brandy provides useful sustenance.

To be fair, life did give Mahler a kick in the guts. When his adored eldest daughter died of scarlet fever in 1907, he was also diagnosed with a life-threatening heart problem. That same year he began his setting of texts based on ancient Chinese poetry, a virtual symphony with solo voices.

Initially called 'The Song of Earthly Sorrow', then renamed *The Song of the Earth*, it is an ocean of Mahler's life philosophy: in the opening 'Drinking Song of Earth's Misery' the key phrase is 'Dark is life, dark is death'. Despite the old Eastern origins, we don't get musical haiku; the setting of the final poem, 'The Farewell' (*Der Abschied*) takes nearly half an hour to perform, longer than all the preceding movements put together. I'm not one for long goodbyes, but this is no mere tear-stained waving on the dock. It makes sadness feel like a privilege.

FREEDOM & RELEASE

'A man of superior talents becomes bad if he always stays in the same place.'
Wolfgang Amadeus Mozart, 1778

*'Profession: Musician-Philosopher
Coming from: Doubt
Journeying towards: Truth'*
Franz Liszt, entry in a hotel register, 1836

Fine for those 'artistic' types, all that flitting about. Composers seem such creatures of whim; they had no compunction about upping sticks and hustling on to the next city where an audience awaited. Travelling minstrels, most of them.

The truth is more mundane. For hundreds of years

composers and performers were considered to be mere crotchet-bearing providores. In palaces and mansions the sonatas were delivered at the back door along with the cabbages. Even Mozart was a low-paid servant for the early part of his career, joining those in a profession who were captives of drudgery: 'a concerto – tomorrow? Of course, your Majesty'. Most of them would have loved to pull out the scissors and cut the suspenders of servile captivity. But a man without suspenders has his pants on the floor.

∼

Snip, Snip

Wolfgang Amadeus Mozart (1756–1791) was one of classical music's free spirits and an astonishing talent; possibly the most naturally and abundantly gifted musician the Western world has ever known. Some time ago a number of psychologists were asked to try and estimate the IQs of history's great creators. Some of the results were astronomically high – I think that Goethe and Michelangelo clocked in at over two hundred apiece – but in the case of Mozart they wouldn't even hazard a punt.

No wonder people were both curious and slack-jawed in the 1760s when the child Mozart was touring Europe with his father and older sister. The facts of his precocity are amazing:

- Mozart was picking out tunes at the keyboard at three and demonstrating perfect pitch at four when telling his elders that their violins were a quartertone out of tune. (That's half of a semitone we can play on the piano.)

- At five he had become a keyboard virtuoso. A year later, his father Leopold began exhibiting him relentlessly around Europe, playing in royal courts and musical academies as well as to the public.

- At seven he picked up a violin, had a think, and played it, even though he'd had no violin lessons.

- At eight he wrote his Symphony No 1 in E flat, K16.

- His first major opera, *La finta semplice*, was premiered when he was thirteen.

From then on Mozart's output was staggeringly prolific, as you see if you scan the Köchel catalogue of his music first compiled in the 1860s: well over six hundred works. It has been estimated that a music copyist working by hand would be hard pressed to write as many notes in the same time.

Mozart worked fast, and he was talented enough to take shortcuts; for instance, he could think out a complete string quartet and write out the individual parts *first* before making the full score, or he could notate a complicated piece on paper while thinking out another piece in his head.

There are plenty of stories like these. When hearing them you just have to give up trying to understand just how such a mind can work, because these are the more obvious acrobatic dimensions of the talent. The real miracle lies in the quality of the work itself, not in these child prodigy days, but in the all-too-short adult phase of his life.

Mozart was 'on the road', so to speak, for about fourteen of his thirty-five years, meaning that he was exposed to all of the stylistic currents in European music-making. It was a patchwork quilt of influences upon which to draw, and his intellect was easily able to absorb all of them. Pulling out the thread of one's own voice can be difficult when such a tapestry is so large, even for a genius, so you have to look to Mozart's mid-twenties before his real musical self emerges. Once that was clarified, the stream of masterpieces is overwhelming, and certainly proved so to many of his contemporaries.

There is the famous testimony by the elder statesman of composers, Joseph Haydn (1732–1809), to Mozart's father in 1785, 'I tell you before God, as an honest man, your son is the greatest composer known to me in person and by name.' Praise indeed for a musician not yet thirty, but the older man was perceptive; by then Mozart had tested and mastered every form of instrumental and vocal music.

Make any generic list you like and he'll be up there somewhere. Symphonies? His last three (numbers 39 to 41) were composed in the summer of 1788 with no prospect of imminent performance; he never lived to hear them. We have made up for it since then as they are now among the most-played symphonies in the world. The first movement of Symphony No 40 in G minor, K550, became a bizarre disco hit in the 1970s, surviving the superimposition of a drum-kit. The finale to the Symphony No 41 in C, K551 (nicknamed 'Jupiter') is the culmination of Mozart's late interest in fugue and counterpoint; the themes slip around each other like mud-wrestlers. The sense of physicality almost overwhelms the listener by the closing bars.

Concertos appealed to Mozart's creativity, with their symbolism of the solo instrument breaking free from the webbing of orchestral accompaniment. My first hearing of a Mozart concerto was that for Flute and Harp (1776), a combination so attractive that I'm surprised more concertos weren't written for this pairing. Many of the keyboard concertos, and he wrote twenty-seven, were 'make-work' exercises for their diminutive composer–virtuoso, who was hungry for performance fees. Solo status apart, Mozart doesn't necessarily allow the piano to have all the fun; the opening of the Concerto No 27 K595 – his last – allocates a profusion of melodies to the orchestra at the start. Lesser composers would trade in their wooden dentures for just one tune in this league, but here's the Austrian handing them out like campaign leaflets.

The middle movement of the Piano Concerto No 21, K467 (1785) became famous as the theme of the sixties film about a tightrope dancer, *Elvira Madigan*; the melody tracing a similarly high arc in Wedgewood blue over a gently-throbbing accompaniment. Pure Rococo 'prettiness', yet there is something else in there, shadows thrown into the music by something just beyond our field of perception.

∼

There is darkness in every personality, and it's hardly revelatory to suggest that in Mozart's case some of this stems from the relationship with his father, Leopold. One doesn't have to be too astute to realise that a childhood like Wolfgang's – the rootlessness, transitory friendships, endless praise from strangers, continuous demands from an exploitative father – is not the best preparation for a responsible adult life.

Mozart was a good son but his dad was a nag: Leopold's mantra was get a good job and keep it. Don't mix with unsavoury people. Look after your money and respect it. Sounds familiar? Of course it does; it's the advice that most parents give to their children. Wolfgang was never about to become a delinquent, but he was headstrong, and the temperamental opposite of his father. Moreover, he was a free-spirited genius, and as such was virtually predestined to let his conservative father down.

The celebration of the free spirit reached an apotheosis in Mozart's operas. He understood the stage, and he understood people, and was able to describe real three-dimensional beings in all their complexity and subtlety for almost the first time in opera. They either chafe inside a system – as does the wily but good-hearted Figaro in *The Marriage of Figaro*, anything but blindly subservient to his employer – or they break free and go exploring for sexual conquest (*Don Giovanni*), the limits of fidelity (*Così fan tutte*) or wisdom (*The Magic Flute*, which also contains Mozart's idea of the parent from hell in the character of The Queen of the Night). In Mozart, the truly free spirit is one that can accept human frailties; his characters forgive each other their misdirected desires, and at the end of *Così* even beg the indulgence of the audience. It is the aristocratic libertine Don Giovanni whose refusal to change his point of view sees his spirit cast into an infernal cage.

Freedom Doesn't Always Work

In 1781, when employment with a wealthy patron was as much as musicians of his day could hope for, Mozart abruptly broke his service with the Archbishop of Salzburg. Being ranked at table below even the valets when travelling with the royal entourage ('at least I have the honour of sitting ahead of the cooks'), as well as the miserable salary, had finally exasperated his sense of self-worth. He also had a headful of music that was not about to be emptied in the course of his employment for a phlegmatic member of the Church.

The decision did not go down well; Mozart's resignation was sealed with 'a kick on my arse by order of our worthy Prince Archbishop'. It was classical music's most fateful boot up the behind, propelling Mozart to the big smoke of Vienna and a new world, a remote world for a musician in those days: that of the freelance musician, the 'gun for hire'. Now he just had to keep his pants up.

Casting your fate to the winds sounds romantic, but it helps to be a little sensible when it comes to the world's mundane matters, such as paying the rent and practising the odd bit of strategic diplomacy. Both are tall orders if you've been brought up as a child prodigy; the expectation is that someone else will take care of such loose ends.

One of the false Mozart legends is that fate and a

jealous circle of enemies deprived him of both money and opportunity. It *is* true that Mozart didn't have much luck with landlords – he moved house eleven times in his last nine years – and he had to beg more than a few florins from friends. But there was usually plenty of money coming in. Even when on his uppers, Mozart still kept servants, stabled a horse in the Vienna Woods for riding every afternoon, and frequently indulged in new clothes; his fellow composer Clementi remarked that Mozart dressed 'like an aristocratic courtier'. We know now that in his final ten years in Vienna, Mozart earned more than most musicians around him, and far more than he could ever have expected to earn back in Salzburg.

So what happened to the money? Mozart wasn't a heavy drinker or gambler; nevertheless, no sooner did the money come in than it was gone, and the detectives among modern musicologists are still trying to trace where. Yes, Mozart could lend to unreliable friends indiscriminately; yes, his wife Constanze was a frequent visitor to some of the fashionable and expensive health resorts to take the waters. But we've still a way to go.

Then there is the mystery of Mozart's sudden death. Early nineteenth-century gossip claimed murder by poison as the cause, with the likeliest suspect being Mozart's rival composer Antonio Salieri (1750–1825). By 1824 the audience at a performance of Beethoven's Ninth Symphony were being handed leaflets describing Salieri standing by Mozart's side with a poisoned cup. Two years later the Russian writer Pushkin enshrined the rumour in the 'dramatic dialogue' *Mozart and Salieri*, later turned into an opera by Rimsky-Korsakov. And of course we have the play *Amadeus* by Peter Schaffer, adapted for the screen with enormous commercial success in 1984.

'So young, so young!' we now cry – but dying at thirty-five wasn't all that unusual in Mozart's time. His was not a pauper's grave; it was a simple unmarked one, as was the lot of most people of the time. It wasn't a rainy day at Mozart's funeral as *Amadeus* portrayed and as would befit the tragedy of neglected genius; the weather report tells us it was quite a pleasant early winter's day. The wrongfully accused Salieri not only followed Mozart's coffin to its resting place on 7 December 1791, he also became the music teacher to Mozart's son, Franz Xaver Wolfgang. This didn't seem to bother Mozart's widow.

Nevertheless – what happened? Mozart was never a particularly robust specimen, and it has been theorised that the composer fell victim to a recurrent and in those days very common streptococcal infection that caused flu symptoms the first time around, and complete renal failure the second, with up to ten years separating the two illnesses. It was a nasty European version of the 'flu'; a shot of penicillin would probably have saved him. We are left with music's greatest 'what if': imagine what Mozart could have done with another thirty-five years. At least we have the *first* thirty-five.

~

There was *one* kind of release that gave Mozart a hearty laugh all his life, and it involved toilet humour. Excretion and all its warning signs are a recurring motif in his jokes with his family. In part this was an element of the kid who never grew up (don't most children get a giggle from a fart?), but it was also a product of his domestic and cultural environment; Salzburg citizens were noted in the 1770s as being 'exceedingly inclined to low humour'.

When I began radio broadcasting on a daily basis, playing classical music to listeners in the early morning, I tended to enthuse about it by explaining my own reactions. This subjective approach polarised the audience for a while, some of whom thought this inappropriate for great music. To them, I was a vandal spraying graffiti on the walls of these temples of perfection.

A marvellous letter of complaint in a newspaper listed various transgressions, the most grave being my presentation of Mozart. In talking about him, she said, I had resorted to 'coarse and vulgar expressions'. (In truth, there may have been a bottom joke.) 'Off the air!' was the concluding war cry.

I took great pleasure in replying that the offending words of the introduction in question had fortunately not been mine; in fact, I had been quoting from one of Mozart's own letters. The vulgarian had been the composer himself.

~

Other Free Spirits

Clément Janequin (c1485–1558) also found himself outside the system back in the days when a regular position in a cathedral or court was *de rigeur*. Early employers kept dying on him and a series of prebends were both short-lived and low-paid (Janequin studied for the priesthood). Masses and motets weren't his 'thing' anyway; he preferred writing secular songs, or *chansons*, with subjects ranging from love to battle, and full of effects: animal impressions, sighs of love, war cries, and the sounds of the elements.

This early musical free spirit was only ever employed sporadically. In his early sixties he enrolled at Paris University as a mature-age student, perhaps to fatten up his educational qualifications for those upcoming job interviews. It was all to no avail. Janequin left little at his death, and what there was went to charity, rather than his family. He had never held an important regular position. Today his *chansons* are sung more widely than ever, but modern-day concert hall settings would have amazed Janequin, who was never happier than when belting out his own tunes in three or four parts with friends around a table.

∽

How free-ranging: a young, longhaired Hungarian-born piano virtuoso elopes from Paris to Switzerland in 1835 with another man's wife. She bears him three children while he further refines an already astonishing keyboard technique and writes music in lakeside villas scented with magnolias.

This is a fragment of the picturesque, and picaresque, life of Franz Liszt (1811–1886) who would quite easily have filled every chapter of this little book. The woman was the Countess Marie d'Agoult; the pair and their occasional retinue of bohemians caused a stir in hotel lobbies everywhere (see Liszt's entry in a register at the beginning of this chapter). His version of freedom was a relationship outside conventional morality pursued in isolated snow-capped surroundings, evening reveries in a gondola, and a disdain for possessions. Marie wrote, 'a bad piano, a few books, the conversation of a serious-minded woman suffice for him'. Later, in Switzerland, Liszt began his collections of pieces, called *Years of Pilgrimage*.

It was too good to last. Despite all this 'freedom', Marie suffered spells of depression and wrote gloomily 'I feel myself an obstacle to his life.' The relationship soured. Liszt embarked on another type of 'freedom' by inventing the modern piano recital and playing concerts all over Europe over a period of nine years from 1838, from Moscow to Lisbon, from Constantinople to Belfast: more than a thousand concerts in all. These were the years of so-called 'Lisztomania' (see *Lust*).

Eventually this life on the road lost its lustre for Liszt. He said, 'always concerts! Always to be a valet of the public! What a trade!' In 1847 he announced his intention of retiring from the concert platform for good and never again played in public for his own benefit. Still only thirty-six years old, he settled down – with a new love, of course.

An even bigger tearaway was the Spaniard Isaac Albéniz (1860–1909). Initially self-taught at the piano, he made his debut in Barcelona when aged four. At seven he was taken to Paris, but came a cropper when caught breaking the windows in his classroom. Back in Spain, he started running away from home, eventually stowing away on a boat to South America, living by his wits and talents all over the continent. He was not yet a teenager. Returning to Europe, he finished off piano studies with Franz Liszt. That classic 'Spanish' sound in piano music owes much to Albéniz.

∼

Wandering and Pilgrimage

The concept of 'the journey' contains many spiritual and metaphysical resonances; *we* are the journey, going through life. 'A stranger I came, a stranger I depart' is the opening phrase of Franz Schubert's late song cycle *Winter's Journey* (1827). The cold starkness of the settings reflects inner and outer landscapes. Berlioz's symphony *Harold in Italy* (1834) describes our Byronic hero's encounters with bandits, lovers and pilgrims, while referring to his inner turmoil, an example of travel's providing the best circumstance for introspection.

This may be one of the reasons why pilgrimages were undertaken in such volume during the Middle Ages. People would leave their homes around Europe to trek to 'holy' places, braving weather, ill health and robbers, never certain that they would see loved ones again. Friendly monasteries would put the travellers up en route. One of them, the shrine of Montserrat near Barcelona, had its monks knock out some tunes for the pilgrims' entertainment before lights out; they were often in high spirits, we're told. Some of the music was collected in a fourteenth-century volume that we call *Libre Vermell*, the 'Red Book' of Montserrat. Seven hundred years later, the melodies still hypnotise.

The region of Galicia in Spain's north-west corner has

been one of the most popular and revered destinations for more than a thousand years; ever since word was enthusiastically leaked out that the remains of Saint James, one of the original band of Christ's disciples, had been discovered by a local bishop on a remote hillside in the area after some divine constellational finger-pointing. From this seed (or more appropriately, those bones) sprang the church, then the monastery, then the city of Santiago de Compostela, attracting countless pilgrims from all over medieval Europe. One of them, a French cleric called Aimery Picaud, documented the main route through Spain in his *Codex Calixtinus* in the mid-twelfth century: probably the first real travel guide.

Pilgrimage seems to have made a comeback in the past couple of decades. Picaud's route, the so-called Camino de Santiago, became the first European Cultural Itinerary in 1987, its 709 kilometres from the Pyrenean foothills to Santiago itself clearly marked for foot-weary modern pilgrims, whose numbers increase every year.

I observed them in clusters by the roadside, or (not infrequently) alone, sunburnt faces turned to the ground and seemingly oblivious to their surroundings, as I passed by in a car going the other way. Not for me the physical ordeal: the blisters, dormitory sleeping quarters in the roadside stops, and pre-dawn starts. I went for a good time, especially one that involved rising late. What bliss!

Eventually I bumbled amiably behind the wheel for some 4,500 kilometres, keeping remarkably true to my original itinerary: Pau (in France), Cantabria, Asturias and Galicia along the Spanish coast to Santiago itself, nowadays a lively university city, its bands of pipe-playing students mingling with the wind-whipped pilgrim arrivals, and most westerly to Cabo Finisterre, the place where the world ended before Columbus (as the word suggests). After travelling to the end of the earth I turned eastwards again and returned to France, stopping along the way at a couple of monasteries for tea, a bunk and an eavesdrop on the monks' ritual sing-along (more about this in *Peace*).

The Harold in both Byron and Berlioz said 'high mountains are a feeling'. My upper thighs proved this as I strode around the Pyrenees for seven days in the company of some Australians, together with a sprinkling of curious locals. The dramatic expenditure of carbohydrates no doubt explained the vigour with which we attacked ducks, rabbits and snails every evening back at our hotel. One afternoon, still glowing from exertion and exhilaration after tackling the monumental Cirque de Gavarnie, a huge curtain of rock on the French–Spanish border, our bus stopped to pick up some hitchhikers: two obviously milk-fed German girls, who explained between fits of giggles that they were also making a pilgrimage to Santiago to try and lose weight. Their laughter was infectious; one of the more senior walkers, visibly moved by the girls' fleshly opulence, turned moist eyes in my direction and confided, 'Ah, Chris, you wouldn't be dead for quids.' It was the most profound utterance of the trip.

Things were equally boisterous in a little hill village further east called Aiglun (population 28), where I met and befriended the local builder, Rocco Rossini, who boasted proudly of his close family ties to the great composer. Certainly he inherited a fondness for the pleasures of the table. All of our conversations took place at *casa* Rossini during long lunches and dinners that merged into each other with barely enough pause for Rocco to shoulder a gun and bring back another wild boar from the surrounding hills (strictly in season, of course). So long, Rocco, and thanks for the *sanglier*.

~

The suspenders have slipped, the mind is emptied, and in following the examples of our distinguished musical predecessors we have arrived at a state of readiness for the new: *Hope*.

Hope

'Pleiades: Kungkarungkara ... Sirius: Warepil ... Crux Australis: Waluwara ...'
Ross Edwards, *Star Chant*, 2001 (text by Fred Watson)

Some time ago, on the other side of my back lane, lived a composer who spent his time writing music for stars – the ones in the sky.

Most mornings I crossed the lane with my two dogs and went around the block so that I could stroll past the front of the house where Ross Edwards lived with his wife Helen and their two kids. He would usually be there in a room overlooking the street, hunched over an electric piano, an enormous corkboard studded with manuscript sheets propped up before him. For a big orchestral work, like a symphony, the acreage of paper was considerable.

On lucky days he would ask me in for a chat and a play-through of the piece in progress.

Ross isn't remotely whimsical in his work patterns. He is a dedicated craftsman who picks up tools at the beginning of what we call 'office hours' and continues well after most of us have adjourned to the pub for end-of-day consolation. Pick, pick, pick at the keyboard: scribble, scribble. Rub out. Rewrite. He must run up quite a bill in pencils; those notes don't just plop onto the paper as if summoned from thin air. A symphony doesn't arrive like fine weather. This looks like hard work to me: real labour. Music is something a composer actually *makes*. Ross is obviously a real composer, so all I can conclude is that the rest of them must have worked their butts off as well.

~

A composer lived on the other side of my back lane. How exotic: I might just as well have written that I keep a living dodo in the cellar. One assumes composers to be a rare species indeed, if not actually extinct. How could those peri-wigged woodland creatures of old have survived in today's world? The chainsaw of economic rationalism has logged their old cultural habitats. Rich people don't keep their own house orchestras busy on a weekly diet of new symphonies any more. The opera-going public isn't clamouring for this month's latest hit. Our society doesn't have the time or money to support artists who insist on producing something so commercially dysfunctional. Television themes, commercial jingles and gaming soundtracks are the pathways of the labourer composer these days; as for the forest of a symphony or the tundra of music theatre – who wants to go there?

The Australian composer Ross Edwards does. In fact, he's never happier than when he's inside a symphony – or a forest, for that matter. Ross can take the sound of a forest and turn it *into* a symphony. His music almost seems to have sprouted from the loam in some isolated gully, pulsing with a sonic sap inspired by the sound of birds and insects encountered during the walks and meditations in the bush. The natural world infuses many of his titles: *Mountain Village in a Clearing Mist*; *Prelude and Dragonfly Dance*; *Raft Song at Sunrise*; *White Cockatoo Spirit Dance*.

Birdsong has cropped up in music over the ages, almost always as quotation. Think of the second movement ending in Beethoven's Sixth Symphony, called the 'Pastoral'. It's like Beethoven standing up during party charades and saying 'here's my imitation of a bird'.

Ross Edwards isn't the charades type. I can't imagine him drawing attention to himself at any party. He doesn't do bush 'impressions'. The listener doesn't sit through an Edwards piece waiting to recognise the grasshopper. No specimens under glass adorn his music's walls. They *are* the walls; sounds from nature re-emerging as musical symbols, bent every which way to create the figurations, contours, rhythms and textures of an ever-expanding body of work.

Ross was born in Sydney in 1943. He has no recollection of a childhood enthusiasm for the heavens, but when commissioned to write his fourth symphony for the 2002 Adelaide Festival after a lifetime of singing about the world, he reached for the stars via an incantatory choral work with a text by the astronomer Fred Watson, listing major stars and constellations as they spin in sequence through an Australian night sky. Their classical names are juxtaposed with the Australian Aboriginal equivalents; Edwards and Watson are both admirers of indigenous cultures. The symphony is called *Star Chant*.

~

This particular morning Ross has ushered me into his workroom. He is a technophobe; nevertheless, concessions have been made to the modern world. One bench top contains a fax machine, a photocopier, a scanner and a PC for emails and regular inspection of his personal website. Ross navigates these functions with the caution and success rate of a learner driver. (Older composers with a more mathematical bent would doubtless have relished the cyber-world. I'm convinced that Mozart would have made a fortune writing software.)

Still, these are merely the flashing lights in a mystic's cave or a forest burrow. Ross has a slight *Wind in the Willows* look about him, despite the tropical shirt. I can see him at the back of Rat's boat, shyly sipping another lemonade or, more likely, a riesling. Slight behind a molehill of embonpoint, tousle-haired, bearded, a soft candour in his eyes, he looks both youthful and avuncular.

Edwards is comfortable in his habitat because it helps him reduce his existence to one purpose. After all, creative artists don't merely toss ideas around in their heads; they often have to bounce them off the walls. This particular room has incubated two symphonies already with a third on the way. Does the music still resonate deep down in those atoms? I remember being in the writing room of Ravel's house outside Paris years before and quietly pressing my ear to an architrave on the off-chance of hearing a faint ripple of the *Pavane for a Dead Princess*. Ravel, being long dead, was not there to disapprove.

Ross is sitting at the piano before his giant corkboard and its tiers of notation. Peering up at the top left corner sheet, he begins to play the opening of his symphony while rendering a Tibetan throat-singer's impression of a choir. I could swear I see stars and check my scalp for any concussion. The music itself has poleaxed me, of course.

It is humbling to be serenaded by a composer with music that no one else has heard. Surely, there is nothing more important going on in the world at this moment. There is integrity to the work that fills the air between us and seals the music's existence irrespective of the number of its future listeners. It is *there*. We have to hope that some will be lucky enough to find it.

What is the best thing to hope for in this life? If composers are any guides, it is to discover one's song and learn to sing it. The search can be agonising. For a lucky few, the knowledge is as obvious as stubbing a toe.

Ross Edwards was aware of music in his head as a child. When he was thirteen he was taken to an orchestral concert and heard music making at this sophisticated level for the first time. He had stubbed his toe. *Two* toes, perhaps spraining his foot, realising at once that there was only one thing he wanted to do, but that he was going to have to work hard to learn how to do it.

Secondary school was no help. Edwards describes his early education as at best 'an inconvenience', at worst 'a concentration camp'. As an only child he was naturally the focus of his parents' highest expectations, and it was thought that young Ross might become an architect. Since architecture has been called 'frozen music', the Edwards family wasn't far off the mark, but the budding composer with some talent for drawing had already chosen bar lines over balustrades.

This was the late fifties in Australia and such a career choice was unorthodox. To be a composer now is still considered exotic; back in the time of Menzies, such bohemian leanings were simply outlandish. Edwards went through conservatoria and universities in Sydney and Adelaide, gaining a Bachelor of Music in 1968 and becoming the star character in a number of musical urban myths that I would love to include here. I had fellow composer Peter Sculthorpe tell some of them for me in a radio documentary I made about Edwards in 1984. Essentially, they are variations on the theme of the absent-minded innocent abroad. Ross swears they're all false, and that my broadcasting them in the first place caused some hurried explanations to his in-laws. I believe him now because the affable woodland creature aura doesn't match such quiet determination.

By the late sixties Edwards was in London, later in an isolated farmhouse in Yorkshire, refining his craft. We're told that ease of expression comes with a developing technique; however, Edwards began to find the opposite to be the case. Alone with his sheets of manuscript paper, he harboured doubts about the direction of all his work up to that moment. He had trapped himself inside the wrong song.

The realisation that one has been going in the wrong direction in life is one of the most terrifying we can have. It is one that many of us avoid because the consequences would be just too harrowing: what happens to the reputation, the self-esteem or the mortgage? Until quite recently, making such a judgement was considered to be capricious and premature if the person was young; for those who were older it was thought of as a symptom of 'mid-life crisis' (see Chabrier in *Joy*). Go back, you are going the wrong way? Nonsense! Once out of the starting blocks, we were not supposed to deviate from the lane boundaries. Anything that involved self-appraisal – or worse, self-*renewal* – was a cop-out. Cop-outs are for wimps.

These days there is a refreshing new awareness that a life can encompass several careers. In the case of a creative artist, 'career' is not the point at issue; it is something more fundamental, more intimate: a judgement about the very core of their being, the point of their existence. When a shadow falls across a lifetime of previous assumptions about oneself, the results can be cathartic. So it was for Edwards, who admits that at the time he was 'physically sick at the thought of some of the music I'd been writing: just torrents of notes saying the world is awful and here I am in it. It was entirely neurotic stuff. I was fighting against a system that I didn't believe in. I was trying to make something work that never could work. I simply realised, you've got to stop doing this.'

From 1974 to 1976 Ross wrote virtually nothing. Now in his thirties and having already had his works performed around Australia and overseas, it was a potentially dangerous situation to be in when strategy might have dictated a speeding-up of activity. Edwards had decided to take a more intuitive approach to his work. 'At this stage,' he says, 'my instincts told me to stop trying.'

Let It Go And It Will Come Back

The stillness that must precede renewal will be familiar to those of a contemplative nature. A two-year stillness is a long hiatus in the early part of a working life. But silence is an important element of Edwards' work, and he gradually began to accept this creative silence as a constructive necessity.

'The solution was for me to learn to relinquish a lot of control,' he says. And in creating this space around himself, fresh messages began to arrive, not from the 'awful' world from which he had felt increasingly alienated, but from the natural world: the bush sounds of birds and insects who were the local minstrels at Pearl Beach on the New South Wales coast where the composer lived with his young family in the late seventies. His true song was all around him.

What emerged from this hibernation were two distinct and contrasting styles. One, his 'sacred' style, takes us deep into the quiet of the soul, a lush silent darkness flecked sparsely by pinpoints of sound. It feels like heresy to have to dwell in these silences in the company of anyone else, which perhaps explains why Ross is uncomfortable with the listening environment of the concert hall with all those people just bursting to cough. It is like taking the delicate fluttering and scuttling of his music and nailing it to a wall. Short of transporting busloads of listeners to the nearest national park and serenading them through an invisible sound system, Ross sometimes requests that the lights in the performance space be dimmed.

Anyway, why be inside a concert hall when you can be on top? His *Dawn Mantras*, first performed before sunrise on New Year's Day 2000 and telecast direct around the globe, perched a young girl singer, a shakuhachi (bamboo flute), two Burmese gongs and a didgeridoo atop the sails of the Sydney Opera House, juxtaposing sounds and cultures in a glorious slow-motion song of hope, arcing as high and wide as the dawning sky above them. For many, it was the highlight of what was otherwise a 24-hour international fireworks display.

The other style is what Ross calls his 'maninya' style. The word sounds vaguely Indonesian to me, but Ross says it is his own invention. Whatever it is, one can't try to pronounce it without inflecting the word with rhythm; likewise, it describes his 'kick yer shoes off and hit the floor' ethos: lightness, spontaneity and the rush to dance. He has written several pieces with the word as their title, the largest of them being his 1988 violin concerto, given the plural *Maninyas*.

Back in my sound producer days I was lucky enough to be entrusted with the studio recording of this work for commercial release with the Sydney Symphony Orchestra, conductor Stuart Challender and soloist Dene Olding. The venture was a success, winning recording awards in Australia and Europe, but whenever I hear it back those fond memories of the working experience are elbowed aside and I marvel at the music all over again.

The score seems to shine from the inside. It pays a ritual homage to the earth with its emphatic but soft-edged pulsing; we are dancing on moss. Fragments of melody are happily reiterated like kids calling each other to play. The middle movement is the reflective flip side of this exuberance; a modern slow plainchant on the violin over a grave processional intoned by low strings. I once conducted this movement in what was essentially a 'comedy' concert in Tasmania. At the music's conclusion I turned to the soloist, only to notice tears streaming down her face. She wasn't laughing.

Edwards doesn't write 'religious' music in the Christian, denominational sense of the term. He has quoted from medieval plainsong, most notably the *Ave Maria, gratia plena* ('Hail Mary, full of grace'), placing Mary at the centre of a more pantheistic belief. To him, she represents 'the universal and eternal feminine spirit, the Earth Mother, source and nurturer of all living things'.

Though I have no idea of Ross' faith at all, I suspect any musings on the hereafter are secondary to his concerns for fixing up the here and now. He assigns a function to his work in a dislocated world, saying that 'it's not only possible, it's *essential* to write music that can rebalance, harmonise and heal instead of music that describes the world we've just come out of. I know it's naive, but you have to have a certain amount of naiveté. Otherwise, you would just go mad.'

Edwards believes that society today has inherited divisions between 'matter and spirit, masculine and feminine, mind and body and so on' (he writes this about his Third Symphony). He also has a hope – better than this, a belief – that we increasingly feel the need for balance and conciliation, which he expresses by 'trying quite consciously to write beautiful music, whereas a few years ago you would have been ostracised for it'.

Ross should know. Much of his work in recent years has met a frosty reception from some fellow composers and the odd critic. Edwards' idea of 'beauty' in music finds an accord with audiences around the world, and this implicit ease of access raises the hackles of some hardheads in the 'serious' music world (many of whose works are played less often, I suspect). According to this lofty fraternity, if the typical concert-goer appears to like a new piece too readily it must be assumed that he or she hasn't had to work too hard to find their way into it; ergo, the composer has 'written down' to them. I must say this constant assumption of the public's stupidity irritates me. Having been privileged to talk to the public for many years in the course of broadcasting, I've learned to admire and respect the sincerity of its response to music that might induce a sneer from some. If you or I are immediately moved by a piece, be it new or old, we don't want that very personal experience invalidated by an accusation that we weren't listening properly, or that the piece must have been too 'easy'. *Really.*

It has always been so. Composers too love having a go at each other, and they are certainly good at it. Musical invective over the ages makes great reading, even when it is misplaced. Tchaikovsky called Brahms a 'giftless bastard'.

Faith

If you believe, then do it with music. That simple tenet has been classical music's most prodigious inspiration. There is hardly a composer in this book who didn't have a crack at a liturgical piece. Many of the masses, motets and processionals that resulted are so beautiful we don't have to go to church to hear them.

Mind you, the Church was protective of its musical treasures. The famous setting of the *Miserere* by Gregorio Allegri (1582–1652) was kept a secret by the papal choir in the Sistine Chapel for hundreds of years. Not a trickle of its polyphony was allowed to escape those Michelangelo-encrusted walls, either in sound or on paper. When the fourteen-year-old Mozart wrote the whole thing out from memory after a single hearing in 1770 he risked excommunication; instead, the amazed Pope Clement XIV awarded him the Order of the Golden Spur. Mozart later discovered his miraculous transcription contained several mistakes.

Johann Sebastian Bach is something close to God for many musicians. He would have been horrified by the comparison, since for him writing music was a way of sending emails upstairs. The overwhelming bulk of his output was composed for liturgical purposes (he was a cantor) and frequently dedicated 'to the Glory of God'.

Composers also exercised their faith through ordination, although becoming a priest in those days was not only a matter of receiving God's summons; it was also a solid career option. Antonio Vivaldi (1678–1741) was known as the 'Red Priest' of Venice on account of his hair colour. An asthmatic who was excused from saying Mass because his wheezing diluted the power of the Word, he was also prone to leaving the altar mid-sentence if an idea for a fugue suddenly struck him. There was no time to waste when it came to composing; his young charges at the Ospedale della Pietà, a home for orphaned or abandoned girls, needed a steady diet of new concertos for their musical education. They must have been pretty good; Vivaldi turned out more than five hundred in his lifetime.

Despite the prowess of his teaching Vivaldi was voted in and out of his job several times by the institution's governors, and in 1737 was censured for conduct unbecoming to a priest. The carrot-topped man of God was too worldly, maintaining an entourage on his frequent travels that included two sisters, one a former singing pupil, the other his 'nurse'. Tongues wagged.

Vivaldi was also a hard and shrewd businessman when it came to doing publishing deals; the dozen collections of his concertos published during his lifetime earned him some very comfortable amounts of cash which he just as quickly spent (on his entourage, presumably). There was certainly nothing left when he expired in the house of a Viennese saddler's widow, his pockets and his reputation in tatters. The wizard of the violin and creator of the *Four Seasons*, the Baroque's biggest contribution to modern restaurant music, was hustled quickly into a pauper's grave.

More devout was one of my favourite monks, the Spaniard Antonio Soler (1729–1783) who composed furiously within the quiet confines of his cloister. His *Fandango* for harpsichord is one of the daffiest keyboard pieces of the eighteenth century, oscillating hypnotically between two chords for all its 450 bars.

Interesting near-priests include Domenico Zipoli (1688–1726), who went off to South America from his native Italy to be a Jesuit missionary (rather like in the film *The Mission*) but expired in Argentina with tuberculosis before receiving his final orders. An arrangement of one of his adagios into a piece called *Elevazione* (Elevation) was one of the most popular works I ever played on the radio.

Giuseppe Tartini (1692–1770) would doubtless have completed his studies for the priesthood had it not been for his skill as a swordsman, his illicit marriage at the age of eighteen, and the fathering of an illegitimate son with his Venetian landlady. Legend has it that the theme of Tartini's most famous violin sonata was played to him in a dream by the Devil – it is called the *Devil's Trill*.

Franz Liszt took minor orders in the Catholic Church in 1865 after a series of personal tragedies, including the early deaths of two of his children, and his long-time mistress' repeatedly unsuccessful attempts to be granted a divorce from her first husband, thereby paralysing their own wedding plans. The despondent pianist–composer was given a suite of rooms by a cardinal in Rome's Villa d'Este, where the once restless sybarite occupied himself by writing religious music. You must try and have a listen to Liszt's rarely performed oratorio *Christus*, written with a limpidity and simplicity worlds away from the thick cascades of his virtuoso keyboard works.

Music is always there when even the most corrupt and despicable cast their eyes heavenward. The courtesan Thaïs finds God one night to the strains of a solo violin in the 1894 opera by Jules Massenet (1842–1912), but the beautiful *Meditation* failed to convince a cool audience at the Paris Opéra premiere. Deciding that the evening needed a little spicing up, the lead soprano Sybil Sanderson flashed her Californian bust, much to the delight of the infatuated composer. Her breasts were apparently the only things about the opera that the critics remembered.

... Or Lack Thereof

Richard Wagner came to believe that music and art could take over when religion lost its potency. The three came together in Wagner's valedictory *Parsifal* (1882), described as a 'sacred stage festival play' by the composer, who further emphasised the sense of ritual in performance by banning audience applause between the first and second acts.

The story revolves around the Holy Grail; Parsifal himself is a Christ-like figure, and 'Faith' even receives its own melodic motif. That Wagner died six months after its premiere should come as no surprise, for the chorus that crowns the work sounds like a transport to heaven. When the dancing stops at my own wake I wouldn't mind the end of *Parsifal* played as a musical chaser.

Towards the end of his life Hector Berlioz described music as one of 'the wings of the soul' (see *Love*). The agnostic composer couldn't be as sure of the soul's destination. The dramatist in Berlioz seized with relish upon the *Dies Irae* section of his 1837 setting of the Requiem Mass in one of music's great cataclysms (as one would expect for the end of the world), but the spiritual elements of the text find no similar fulfilment. There is no reassurance about life's mystery, no attempted explanation; the only certainty is that of the grave.

One of the most extraordinary moments occurs in the *Hostias*, only forty-seven bars long, intoned as a chordal chant by the men in the chorus, accompanied by low trombones and high flutes. The effect is of whispering harmonics over a pedal note – but it is more unsettling, even sinister than that. Berlioz does not permit us the beatific certitude of a Bach or triumphant resolve of a Beethoven. Years later, he would quote from Shakespeare's *Macbeth* at the head of his own *Mémoires*: 'Life's but a walking shadow . . .', but already in the emptiness of the *Hostias* he makes us peer into the void.

Music As Hope

A famous example of music's restorative powers occurred in 1737 when King Philip V of Spain was suffering from such a long-term depression that he was neglecting affairs of state; he had even stopped shaving, *Dios mio*. After numerous futile attempts to lift his spirits, his wife arranged for the famous Italian castrato Farinelli to knock out a couple of numbers in the royal apartments. The music and the beauty of the singer's surgically preserved soprano did the trick, and the King's stubble was quickly removed. Farinelli's musical cure became instantly addictive. He had to serenade the King with the same four songs every night for the next twenty years.

At the end of Stanley Kubrick's film *2001: A Space Odyssey*, the majestic opening to Richard Strauss' 1896 symphonic poem *Thus Spake Zarathustra* (*Also sprach Zarathustra*) bursts from the screen as a Star-Child still in embryo floats out of the cosmos and casts a benign gaze over the earth. Whatever it means, the image suggests hope and regeneration. I don't know if this enigmatic visitor is named in Ross Edwards' *Star Chant*. It does feel good, though, when creative artists finally decide to join scientists in returning the imagined stare from out there.

∽

It is early evening, and I have made arrangements to cross the back lane to the Edwards' for drinks and stir-fry. Helen Edwards has just rung. Ross is having a productive day with the Fourth Symphony; could we delay the start of dinner for a short while? He is 'bringing in the horns'. I suspect that I'll never be able to hear the Symphony in future without feeling hungry.

∼

Our guide now draws up to the long final chord and a destination beyond the stars. Even hope can be covetous when it is rashly indulged. It is time to leave our emotions behind us.

Peace

We come to our final blissful chapter like a weary traveller at the end of the journey, having been whipped raw by the succession of emotional extremes endured by our noble crew of fools for love. It is time for rest – time for *swooning*.

This is the point where words will simply not do. I was tempted to take a Zen approach here and include several blank pages, culminating with *The End* in very small print on the back flyleaf. It would have allowed you space to record your own reactions to music that takes you to a special place. Instead, I will share with you some of mine, but first you must meet the Ultimate Peace tour guide.

> *'Thus am I, a small feather from the ground commanded to fly.'*
>
> Hildegard of Bingen (1098–1179)

SWOONING

A beautiful image – and the Abbess Hildegard was full of them. They came to her as visions that she eventually wrote down in a book called *Scivias*, or 'Know the Ways'. I call her a guide, and so she was: a guide, a confidante, an adviser, a diplomat and a correspondent for popes, kings and emperors around medieval Europe. They wanted to know the ways in practical and spiritual matters, and the woman known in succeeding centuries as the 'Sybil of the Rhine' appeared to be getting their answers from an impeccable source. 'It is said that you are raised to Heaven, that much is revealed to you, and that you bring forth great writings and discover new manners of song,' wrote one Master Odo of Paris in an 1148 fan letter. In fact, her fan club was enormous; Hildegard of Bingen was the most famous and influential woman of her time.

Another millennium has rolled by since then and we are singing her songs more than ever. Is this because we are newly inspired by their devotional content? Not entirely, although we live at a time when the frantic pursuit of materialism is losing some of its glamour, and there is plenty of modern devotional music in various liturgies that fails to match the exalted sentiments contained within their texts. No – we sing the music of Hildegard because it is some of the greatest music ever written. If her messages were indeed of divine origin, one can only say that she had a good connection.

'Getting' Peace

Arriving at the state of perceiving life that Hildegard managed to sustain seems to me one of the best things we can do for ourselves. The effort of trying to get there is what counts, and the techniques are as wide-ranging as the gap between East and West, as numerous as the religions, cults, gurus and meditation retreats that proliferate around the world.

Hildegard operated within the Christian tradition, and the magnificent poetry with which she expresses her visions abounds in Christian symbolism: old and new 'wine' can represent the Testaments, Mary can be 'the greenest branch', God's love the 'heat of the sun' blazing in a dark sanctuary, Christ's love a 'latticed window', The Holy Ghost, a dove. They are beautiful, lush, richly coloured images.

And they're in Latin, of course. Understanding the text is essential as a devotional aid if Christian worship is your way 'up'. But if all Latin is Greek to you, or you simply cannot read the poetry while your eyes are closed in meditation, Hildegard's music is a marvellous vehicle in itself. She gathered her melodies in the *Symphonia armonie celestium revalationum* ('Symphony of the Harmony of Celestial Revelations'). They are pure melody, unaccompanied, unadorned, a single strand of sound that embodies all thought and encloses the whole spirit and body as it is produced. At least, that is the ideal. It is not just a song; it is a device for meditation, called plainchant. The music is intended to be *used*, rather than overheard. That is why I become tetchy when it is served up as an accompaniment to dinner parties these days. (I'm actually pretty relaxed about classical muzak, believing that most composers would be delighted with the royalties if they were still alive. Schubert won't be harmed by having his 'Unfinished' Symphony heard in a lift.)

Hildegard was the tenth child of a German noble family; as such, she was promised to the Church. By the age of eight she was packed off to begin her novitiate with a nearby recluse, Jutta of Spanheim, who lived in a stone cell. Eight! That was the extent of medieval vocational guidance. Fortunately, she took to the contemplative life like a duck to water – she might have said like a dove to lattice – and one could ponder whether her achievement would have been anywhere near as considerable if she'd simply been married off to some princeling down the road.

She took the veil at fourteen and became the prioress of Jutta's order of nuns upon the latter's death in 1136. Five years later, now entering middle age (a reasonable span already in the Middle Ages, when middle age was about twenty-five) she saw flames descend upon her from Heaven and felt she should get a move on. Thereafter,

Hildegard founded her own monastery in the Rhine valley near Bingen with eighteen other sisters and devoted herself to creativity, writing down her visions in poetry and music, hagiography, and treatises on natural history and medicine. This breadth of vision is hard to reconcile with a woman who had spent her life up to this point in a cell saying nothing much to a recluse. Today, people spend their lives in a small room saying nothing at all to a television set but fail to develop similar intellectual interests.

After Hildegard's death in 1179 four popes initiated processes that would have led to her canonisation. The last was John XXII (1316–1334) but things slowed down after that, probably at the wrong end of an in-tray. Finally, in 2012, Pope Benedict XVI named her a Doctor of the Catholic Church, which in many quarters is considered equivalent to sainthood. Saint Hildegard even has a feast day; give her a thought on 17 September.

There was nothing remotely sinister about Hildegard's visions, no twisting or foaming on the floor, no eyes rolling back in the head at midnight. It was a peaceful process, almost like the miraculous imposition of an alternate reality around her.

Peaceful Recommendations

Piano Quintet No 2 in C minor, Op 115 (Fauré)

The older I become the more this strikes me as one of the greatest pieces ever written. Gabriel Fauré lived a good long span; he was born in 1845 and died in 1924, composing right through to the end. The Second Quintet is one of the very last things he wrote, and to my ears every minute of his life experience is inside it. Or is it every minute of *my* life experience? If music is something like an X-ray mirror with those innermost parts of ourselves bouncing out of the sound, then we all face the delightful prospect of coming to appreciate and understand great music purely because our self-knowledge has increased.

This second Piano Quintet sounds to me as if he has collected the memories of his many life mistakes, accepted their necessity, and then let them go. The music doesn't look heavenward as in his much earlier *Requiem*, where the serenity feels a little drugged, death a matter of going to sleep. The Quintet is more truly valedictory; after all, the composer was in his mid-seventies when he wrote it.

I remember its use in a 1984 film called *A Sunday in the Country* directed by Bertrand Tavernier. An aged artist sits in his *atelier* as the sun sets on a day of family drama. Widowed and alone, aware of his declining powers and the limit of his talent, he peers through the dusk at an incomplete still life on his easel, then at the liver spots on his wrinkled hands. The camera quietly cuts away from the artist's contemplation and drifts slowly to the view over his lush garden from an open window. At the end of the day, at the end of the struggle, all that remains – if we are well-intentioned, diligent and lucky – is a little piece of beauty. Fauré's music says this to me as it flows through this last wordless scene. It is always a privilege to taste the fruit of a life that has been fully resolved through living. On his deathbed, three years after the second Quintet's premiere, Fauré said 'I did what I could.'

Concerto grosso in G minor, Op 6 No 8 (Corelli)

The Baroque period is often cited as being the place for classical music neophytes; all that 'clarity' of texture and driving rhythm supposedly bearing some affinity with much of the popular music of today. This may well be the case, although I recall as a ten-year-old submitting my Beatles-drenched ears to Bach's first couple of Brandenburg Concertos and having no idea of what was going on. I had spent my childhood with 'vertical' music, a single (and frequently wonderful) tune strung like electrical cable between solid harmonic poles. On the other hand, Bach's music was entirely 'horizontal', containing several different melodies all going at the same time, like simultaneous babble from six people at the next table in a foreign restaurant. The ear soon learns to delight in such combinations.

Putting these doubts aside, I always recommend the *concerti grossi* (an early form of the concerto) by the Italian master violinist Corelli (1653–1713). He's an obvious candidate for inclusion in this chapter on the sole basis of his first name, which was Arcangelo, or 'Archangel'. What a brilliant opening line that would have been at a Roman party in the 1670s: 'Hi there, gorgeous, guess my name and I'll take you to Heaven.' Actually, he was named after his father, who had died (and presumably joined that celestial rank) a month before the composer's birth.

Corelli had a serene countenance until he picked up his violin, when all facial hell would break loose, red eyeballs rolling 'as if in an agony'. His diabolical performance manner was contrasted by his compositions, which an eighteenth-century writer described as 'chaste'. Chastity is probably a useful quality to bring to a musical evocation of Christ's birth in this concerto from his posthumously published set of Opus 6 (Corelli was possibly the least prolific of the really great composers).

The *Pastorale* with which the work ends sounds like a rustic shepherd's song over a droning accompaniment; a stained-glass version of what folk music of the time must have been like. Corelli may have been inspired by the music of the Abruzzi shepherds outside Rome who would come into town to celebrate the Christmas festival, but it's more likely he was just being fashionable, writing in a genre that celebrated the apparent purity and simplicity of rural life. Fashion is always badmouthed by unsuccessful artists, though its origins seem quite reasonable to me: the repetition *ad nauseam* of a publicly endorsed idea. Since Corelli was both successful *and* wealthy in his career, fashion was just another convenient conduit to public acceptance. When you're as good as he was the talent shines through anyway.

I may be just a modern sentimentalist when I say the *Pastorale* captures the stillness and magic of that first Christmas Eve in the ancient world. A more cautious compliment then: the music catches the moment and place as we would like them to have been.

The Enchanted Lake (Liadov)

One of the most peaceful of fantasies is that of solitude in a place removed from the importuning 'real' world. Some go to retreats; here is such a musical place. Anatoly Liadov (1855–1914) was perhaps the laziest composer ever, so for him to have finished this short work at all represents a major commitment. In fact, he makes it twice as long as it could have been by repeating each of its ideas like an incantatory echo.

Beam Me Up, Virila

If you're looking for peace, a monastery is hard to beat. Hildegard would agree. In modern Spain one doesn't need to beg for refuge from uncomprehending monks; no, several monasteries have hotel annexes with actual reception desks and credit card facilities where rooms can be had at comparatively modest prices. Spartan they may be but, when at their home, do as the monks do.

I have stayed in two of these Spanish Heavenly Hotels, both in isolated spots: Valvanere, a twelfth-century building in the verdant foothills of the Sierra de la Demanda midway between the cities of Burgos and Logrono; and Leyre, an even older building further to the north-east of Spain in the very American Wild West–looking area of Navarre. It's been said of the latter that one of its eighth-century bishops, one San Virila, constantly prayed for a glimpse of infinity and was granted his wish by a sleep-inducing bird-call that nodded him off for three hundred years.

The monastery has been occupied and run only since 1950 by the Benedictines, who are renowned in Spain for the quality of their plainchant singing. I know this because the winsome reception clerk told me as I checked in. Better still, evensong was starting in five minutes!

Off I rushed to the grand but gloomy church above its pre-Romanesque crypt, my arrival boosting the all-tourist congregation to five. When the clock struck overhead, I was suddenly plunged back into the Middle Ages; thirty monks dutifully shuffled into the chancel, lit their candles and lined up in opposing rows before singing a complete service heavenward in the flickering light. The sincerity in their voices was so moving that I paid no attention to their technical quality. My recollection is that it was pretty good. More than that, it was the moment when in a strange place I didn't feel strange at all. Peaceful, perhaps.

∽

Ah, Hildegard. What a combination: on the one hand an extraordinary focus of creative energy, an intellectual force bursting through the walls of a medieval monastery, rushing down the Rhine and sweeping up admirers in the courts and cloisters of Europe; on the other, a life given to devotion and a prescribed passivity in her self-description as a mere feather drifting on God's breath. There is wisdom in words spoken softly, and then only rarely.

Hildegard never knew the clamour and bustle of secular life, the desperate aspirations of commerce, or sexual love, designer fashion, international travel. She would have disciplined herself to resist most of the emotions we have explored in this book, excepting, of course, Love and a quiet Joy. These are subsumed into her poetry and song, and it's because her music is such an irreducible essence of sound that we feel it embodies some ultimate, necessary Truth. What the Truth is – well, that is up to you; Hildegard of Bingen obviously had a few suggestions.

Coda

'The song is ended but the melody lingers on.'

Irving Berlin, *Ziegfeld Follies*, 1927

When a concert or recital is over it is customary to retire to the bar for a drink. When a love affair is over it is common to take to drink. Some conversation is also involved, although the latter circumstance invites more of a monologue. This is because we feel that our follies are unique.

Music is one of the great barometers of our progress and growth through life. Like aural souvenirs, it can be forever associated with watershed moments in our personal existence, but it also lets us know when we're ready to move on to the next destination in the big spiritual tour. The composers, our fellow travellers, have been there before. But theirs is not an exceptional journey;

or rather, it's as exceptional as the one we all experience.

Artists teach us nothing. They simply point out to us the things we already know. I never expect 'wisdom' from classical music. If anything, I relish the confirmation that most of the composers were as ill-informed and 'un-lived' as I often feel. A year before the premiere of his complete *Ring* cycle in 1876, the 62-year-old Richard Wagner is alleged to have said, 'I know nothing at all about music.' We would all kill to be as ignorant as Wagner. Unfortunately no one can discover the real limits of their knowledge overnight. It takes a lifetime of crashing into reality's walls.

Therefore I hope you take heart from some of the crashes documented here. The path through life is certainly ours to navigate, but if you listen carefully you can hear the snapping of branches and cursing of nearby walking disasters. The woods are alive. What a joy, then, that some of those disasters halted their blind progress now and then to sing us a song.

We are destined to repeat our follies *ad infinitum* because we are human. Soon it will be time to turn back these pages to the start for more counsel as that loop of emotion comes around to start another cycle.

Keep *Swooning* by the bed for reference by all means, but let me conclude (as do many pieces of music in 'sonata' form) with a restatement of the first subject. Now that you've tarried a little on this brackish, pot-holed shoreline, have a little splash in the grand oceanic Real Thing. Listening to some of the music mentioned here will negate those maxims about the futility of trying to write about it. If this indulgent roam through the lives of some musicians suggests the humanity and generosity at the bottom of their collective creative impulse, I'll be delighted. Tackling Beethoven's Fifth will still be your challenge – but you'll never look at his portraits the same way again.

www.ingramcontent.com/pod-product-compliance
Lightning Source LLC
Chambersburg PA
CBHW031807220426
43662CB00007B/551